W9-BCY-498

Thinking Critically:
Social Networking

Jamuna Carroll

ReferencePoint
Press®

San Diego, CA

ReferencePoint
Press®

About the Author

Jamuna Carroll has a bachelor's degree in writing and mass communication. Her writing appears in more than forty books on science, math, civil liberties, and history, as well as humor books. She performs at storytelling events and comedy shows in Southern California, where she shares a vintage house with her partner and daughter.

© 2018 ReferencePoint Press, Inc.
Printed in the United States

For more information, contact:
ReferencePoint Press, Inc.
PO Box 27779
San Diego, CA 92198
www.ReferencePointPress.com

Picture Credits:
All charts and graphs by Maury Aaseng

LIBRARY OF CONGRESS CATALOGING-IN-PUBLICATION DATA

Name: Carroll, Jamuna, author.
Title: Thinking Critically: Social Networking/by Jamuna Carroll.
Description: San Diego, CA: ReferencePoint Press, [2018] | Series: Thinking Critically | Audience: Grade 9 to 12. | Includes bibliographical references and index.
Identifiers: LCCN 2017037299 (print) | LCCN 2017049745 (ebook) | ISBN 9781682823422 (eBook) | ISBN 9781682823415 (hardback)
Subjects: LCSH: Online social networks—Juvenile literature. | Social media—Juvenile literature.
Classification: LCC HM742 (ebook) | LCC HM742 .C357 2018 (print) | DDC 302.30285—dc23
LC record available at https://lccn.loc.gov/2017037299

Contents

Foreword

"Literacy is the most basic currency of the knowledge economy we're living in today." Barack Obama (at the time a senator from Illinois) spoke these words during a 2005 speech before the American Library Association. One question raised by this statement is: What does it mean to be a literate person in the twenty-first century?

E.D. Hirsch Jr., author of *Cultural Literacy: What Every American Needs to Know*, answers the question this way: "To be culturally literate is to possess the basic information needed to thrive in the modern world. The breadth of the information is great, extending over the major domains of human activity from sports to science."

But literacy in the twenty-first century goes beyond the accumulation of knowledge gained through study and experience and expanded over time. Now more than ever literacy requires the ability to sift through and evaluate vast amounts of information and, as the authors of the Common Core State Standards state, to "demonstrate the cogent reasoning and use of evidence that is essential to both private deliberation and responsible citizenship in a democratic republic."

The *Thinking Critically* series challenges students to become discerning readers, to think independently, and to engage and develop their skills as critical thinkers. Through a narrative-driven, pro/con format, the series introduces students to the complex issues that dominate public discourse—topics such as gun control and violence, social networking, and medical marijuana. Each chapter revolves around a single, pointed question such as Can Stronger Gun Control Measures Prevent Mass Shootings?, or Does Social Networking Benefit Society?, or Should Medical Marijuana Be Legalized? This inquiry-based approach introduces student researchers to core issues and concerns on a given topic. Each chapter includes one part that argues the affirmative and one part that argues the negative—all written by a single author. With the single-author format the predominant arguments for and against an issue can be synthesized into clear, accessible discussions supported by details and evidence including relevant facts, direct quotes, current examples, and statistical illustrations. All volumes include focus questions to guide students as they read each pro/con discussion, a list of key facts, and an annotated list of related organizations and websites for conducting further research.

The authors of the Common Core State Standards have set out the particular qualities that a literate person in the twenty-first century must have. These include the ability to think independently, establish a base of knowledge across a wide range of subjects, engage in open-minded but discerning reading and listening, know how to use and evaluate evidence, and appreciate and understand diverse perspectives. The new *Thinking Critically* series supports these goals by providing a solid introduction to the study of pro/con issues.

Social Networking

Worldwide, social networking is used by about 2.5 billion people—one-third of the global population. It has become essential in everyday life for most people. This is especially true for the millennial generation, people born from roughly 1980 to 2000, who are the first to have grown up with social networking. Its importance is exemplified in a blog post by a young Los Angeles music studio intern, who says she is "hooked" on social media. To challenge herself, she swears off social networking for twenty-four hours. She describes how her day starts at 8:00 a.m.: "After rolling out of bed, it feels weird not checking my Snapchat." Throughout the day, she fights the desire to use social networking. She writes, "4 p.m.—I'm realizing the magnitude of social media in my daily routine. Let me check Instagram really quick. Nope . . . 6 p.m.—I decide to go to Malibu and watch the sunset. This is the first time in months I didn't take an Instagram picture or Snapchat the beach scenery."[1] Even when she awakens in the middle of the night, she has the urge to check all her accounts. This young lady's social media usage is not unusual. As more people turn to social media for a wider variety of activities throughout each day, the average Internet user now spends more than two hours a day on social networking sites, according to research by GlobalWebIndex in 2016. Social networking is influencing the way people think, communicate, and interact. Whether these changes are overall beneficial or harmful is hotly debated.

Social Networking Is Wide Reaching

Social networking is so named because it offers members the ability to create personal profiles and share thoughts, photos, videos, or links with other people. Examples include Facebook, Twitter, Google+, and Tumblr. Some social media platforms are more narrowly tailored to users' interests. For example, there are sites to share photos, such as Instagram; video-sharing platforms like YouTube; craft-oriented sites like Pinterest; career sites; dating sites; and more. Around the world, the most widely used social networking site is Facebook, which has over 2 billion users. In North America, 170 million people log on to Facebook every day. Much of this user base is made up of young people. A poll by the Pew Research Center in 2015 shows that 76 percent of teenagers use social media. Among them, Facebook and Instagram are most popular, with 71 percent of teens using Facebook and 52 percent using Instagram. One thirteen-year-old girl from New Jersey said of her social media use with her friends: "We're on it 24/7. It's all we do."[2] Even younger kids have an online presence. Though the minimum age for social media sites (including Facebook) is thirteen, more than half of children under age eleven have used them. The fastest-growing population on social media, though, is not young people, but those over age sixty-five. In 2016, 35 percent of people in this demographic had accounts, most often to stay connected with their grandchildren.

Multiple Uses

Although social networking began in the 1990s for socializing, its uses today are almost limitless: sharing safety information, how-to videos, business presentations, advertisements, and much more. Significantly, for 62 percent of Americans, social media is the source of their news, with Reddit and Facebook being the most common. For communication, too, social networking is becoming the preferred mode for many people, even more so than talking face-to-face. By some estimates, cell phones are now used almost twice as much for social media communication as for phone calls.

Because it is used for so many communications, social networking has the ability to create a permanent record of each user. For instance, other users can take a screen shot, download, or reshare posts or photos even if the original poster deletes them. Moreover, some sites, including Facebook, save backup copies that exist for some time after content

Global Growth of Social Media Users

Social media use is growing on a global scale. According to the report "Digital in 2017: Global Overview," the world had 2.8 billion social media users in 2017. Between January 2016 and January 2017 alone, active social media users increased by 21 percent, or 482 million people worldwide. The highest growth during that period occurred in Saudi Arabia, which experienced a 73 percent rise in the number of people using social media. The more modest growth experienced by countries such as the United States and Canada was largely a result of already high numbers of active social media users.

Increase in the Number of People Using Social Media in Each Country, January 2016 to January 2017

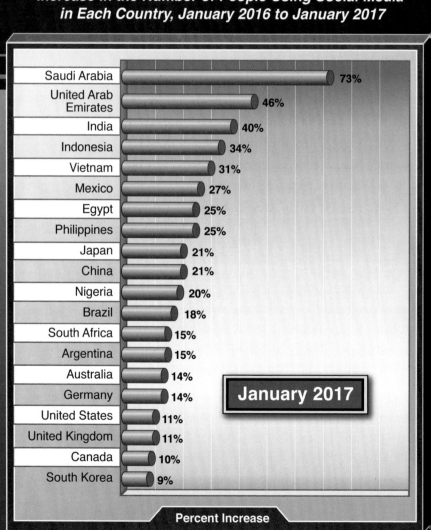

Country	Percent Increase
Saudi Arabia	73%
United Arab Emirates	46%
India	40%
Indonesia	34%
Vietnam	31%
Mexico	27%
Egypt	25%
Philippines	25%
Japan	21%
China	21%
Nigeria	20%
Brazil	18%
South Africa	15%
Argentina	15%
Australia	14%
Germany	14%
United States	11%
United Kingdom	11%
Canada	10%
South Korea	9%

January 2017

Percent Increase

Source: Simon Kemp, "Digital in 2017: Global Overview," We Are Social and Hootsuite, January 24, 2017. https://wearesocial.com.

is deleted. This can be frustrating for users who wish to remove risqué photos or embarrassing posts. Some college applicants have been rejected after their posts about drinking were found, for example. On the other hand, social media's permanence does have some benefits. Police investigators, for instance, find a lot of useful information on social media—including material that has been deleted. This occurred in the case of a Stanford University student who shared a photo of the topless, unconscious woman he had sexually assaulted. Though someone deleted the original message, authorities saw a response to it that helped determine the timing of the assault and prove that the man knew the woman was unconscious when he took the picture.

As in the Stanford case, social networking plays a key role in solving crimes, as well as getting an education, seeking a job, keeping family ties, and providing a voice for people who are depressed or marginalized. Yet at the same time, its detractors argue that social networking destroys people's social skills and mental health, gives rise to bullying, and presents other dangers that make its impact mostly negative.

Social Media's Impact on the 2016 Election

What both sides *can* agree on is a notion expressed by tech columnist Farhad Manjoo: "Across the planet, social networks are helping to fundamentally rewire human society."[3] These words, written about how social networks influenced the 2016 presidential election, highlight the significance of social media. Donald Trump, considered the underdog during the campaign, extolled the virtues of social media for helping him achieve a surprise win. He reached more voters, and at a fraction of the cost, than the other contenders did. He explains, "The fact that I have such power in terms of numbers with Facebook, Twitter, Instagram, et cetera—I think it helped me win all of these races where they're spending much more money than I spent."[4]

After the election, social media expert Karen Yankovich evaluated Trump's campaign. In her calculation, "Twitter has been Trump's biggest platform for social media campaigning. Since he announced he was running for President, Trump gained almost 10 million more followers and has been re-tweeted over 3.5 million times." Even when he sometimes tweeted a claim that seemed unbelievable or offensive, Yankovich maintains it benefited him by driving people to his profile: "Trump's outlandish statement spread his face all over the internet, and the result was the funneling of more people to his page (supporters or not)."[5] Yankovich also credits the fact that Trump, not a campaign manager, wrote his own posts, which she says lent him credibility.

On the other side, commentators have charged that social media contributed to Democratic nominee Hillary Clinton's loss. Not only was she not as successful at drawing online fans as Trump was, but pundits contend that social media algorithms allowed people to widely disseminate false news stories that hurt her campaign. Prior to the election, for example, many stories that made fraudulent claims about her were shared, and the more users who read them, the more the stories were bumped up to prominent places on social media sites where people would see them. A Republican legislative aide, Cameron Harris, admits that weeks before the election, he fabricated a "breaking news" story alleging that tens of thousands of fake ballots cast for Clinton were found. The story, which accused Clinton's campaign of fraud, was shared 6 million times by social networkers who believed it, mainly because it played on fears that Trump gave rise to when he claimed during speeches, "I'm afraid the election is going to be rigged."[6]

Most Clinton supporters blame these stories for scaring off her potential voters. Clinton avers, "Through an enormous investment in falsehoods, fake news, call it what you will—lies—the other side [Trump's campaign] was using content that was just flat out false. . . . If you look at Facebook, the vast majority of the news items posted were fake."[7] Citing this example, some commentators argue that social networking sites should protect users by banning false or otherwise harmful content. However, social media's advocates claim that would destroy the open sharing of ideas for which it is known, and that sites should not decide what content is credible.

Changing Ideas of Privacy

Agreement over what site administrators should do to protect users' privacy is often just as difficult to reach. Social media users share a lot of information about themselves, and even more data is collected by the site, including what articles they read, what products they like, and even their psychological state. For example, Facebook has shown marketers how it analyzes posts to identify teens who feel insecure, worthless, or defeated. Because Facebook and other sites sell the information they gather on users to advertisers, dozens of nonprofit groups accused Facebook of enabling marketers to target vulnerable teens. Another argument is that sharing people's metrics without their knowledge violates their privacy. Others counter that information sharing allows marketing content to be narrowly focused on users who benefit from it, such as showing a news story or advertisement about something they have expressed interest in before. As it turns out, most people are no longer concerned about shielding their information from advertisers. A poll by Microsoft in 2015, for example, found that 99 percent of consumers will give their personal data to companies in exchange for rewards. Compared to surveys from 1989, when 78 percent of consumers felt that companies' online collection of their data was a somewhat or very serious threat to privacy, it seems that notions of privacy are evolving.

Clearly, social media's effects are fundamentally changing people and society. Whether the impact is adverse or beneficial remains to be seen—but social networking will likely continue to grow exponentially in both popularity and function.

Chapter One

Does Social Networking Benefit Society?

Social Networking Is Beneficial to Society

- Through social networking, users can share information and solutions quickly and easily.
- Social networking can provide the motivation and means for political change.
- Campaigns to raise awareness and money for causes are conducted through social networking.
- Social networking connects job candidates with companies and helps people, especially women, further their careers.

The Debate at a Glance

Social Networking Harms Society

- The free flow of information via social networking makes it easy to spread false and dangerous information.
- The multitasking that is required while social networking causes people to have short attention spans and weak critical-thinking skills.
- Distractions caused by social media are harming society.
- Social networking perpetuates bias and racism.

Social Networking Is Beneficial to Society

"Knowing how to use [social networks] can significantly improve the way we communicate, do business, study, inform ourselves and help others."

—Damian Wolf, technology writer

Damian Wolf, "7 Reasons Why Social Networking Is Good for Our Society," Techno FAQ, April 27, 2015. www.technofaq.com.

Consider these questions as you read:

1. How convincing is the argument that social media helps keep the public informed about news, health, and safety information? Cite evidence to support your answer.
2. Have you ever used social networking to share your opinion or support for a political or social cause? Can you think of a situation in which you might? Explain your answer.
3. While some job seekers have been hired based on information discovered in their social media profiles, other companies have decided *not* to hire candidates because of their social media accounts. Do you think social media is more likely to hurt or help job seekers? Explain your answer.

Editor's note: The discussion that follows presents common arguments made in support of this perspective, reinforced by facts, quotes, and examples taken from various sources.

Only a few decades ago, information seekers had to visit a library or ask an expert. Now social networking provides answers instantly to anyone with Internet access, even in the most remote locations. This helps promote public safety, fuel political and social movements, and expand job options, all leading to a better informed, more productive society.

Free-Flowing Information

Social media sites are instrumental in information sharing. A 2016 survey by the Pew Research Center found that 62 percent of American adults get their news from social media. Among millennials, it is 88 percent, according to the American Press Institute. Conveniently, social media news feeds present information automatically without users having to search for it. As a result, marketing expert AJ Agrawal asserts, "News outlets can share breaking stories, alerts and other important bits of news instantly with their followers. When more people are aware of a situation, those working to secure locations and ensure the safety of the general public can perform their job duties more efficiently."[8] Even more impressive is the ability of social networking sites to tailor content to each user. Algorithms based on factors such as what users have "liked" in the past and posts their friends "like" filter out news they are not interested in and prioritize what they are most likely to read.

The sharing of health and safety information is unprecedented, too. Reaching thousands of people at once, posts from health organizations may encourage people to get vaccinations or avoid disease outbreaks. The Centers for Disease Control and Prevention hosted a Twitter chat, for instance, to debunk dangerous rumors about the Ebola virus in 2014. During disasters, social media has saved lives. In 2017, Hurricane Harvey caused massive floods that displaced tens of thousands of Texans. More than a dozen 911 call centers were submerged, making it impossible for many people caught in the rising waters to get through to 911 operators. Even those who did reach emergency dispatchers waited hours or days for help. Panicking and at risk of drowning, some residents used social media to post their status, address, and even photos of their dire situations, which their friends reshared until volunteers with a boat came to rescue them. Other people started Facebook groups to organize rescues of families and their pets from rooftops and attics.

During crises like these, social networks also let people know their friends are safe. In 2016, when a man began shooting at a gay nightclub called Pulse in Florida around two o'clock in the morning, the club posted on its Facebook page, "Everyone get out of pulse and keep running."[9]

Jobvite, a company that produces job recruiting software, interviewed recruiters about their use of social networking in the hiring process. It found that the vast majority—92 percent—use social media to vet job candidates. Social networks are second only behind personal referrals as a means of finding the best job candidates.

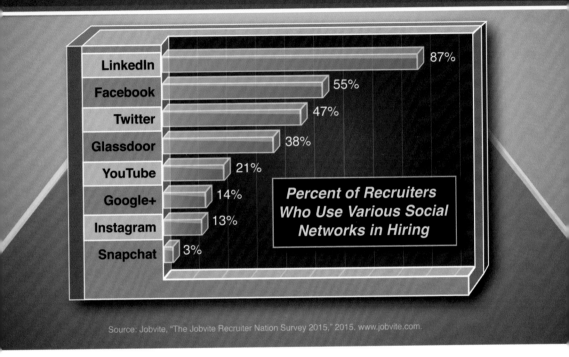

LinkedIn 87%
Facebook 55%
Twitter 47%
Glassdoor 38%
YouTube 21%
Google+ 14%
Instagram 13%
Snapchat 3%

Percent of Recruiters Who Use Various Social Networks in Hiring

Source: Jobvite, "The Jobvite Recruiter Nation Survey 2015," 2015. www.jobvite.com.

The status was shared more than fourteen thousand times, and survivors and witnesses posted updates until the ordeal ended at five o'clock in the morning. Later, the forty-nine people tragically killed were memorialized through social media.

Unfortunately, not all news shared via social networking is useful; false information is sometimes spread, but Google and Facebook have taken steps to counter this. As of 2016, both prohibit fake news websites from using their advertising platforms, which withholds valuable revenue from those sites. In addition, Facebook apologized and promised to do better at filtering fake stories have slipped into its popular Trending topics section. In 2017 a spokesperson assured Facebook's members, "We're working to make our detection of hoax and satirical stories quicker and more accurate."[10]

Political Revolution

Around the globe, social networking is providing the motivation and means for political change. In Ukraine it played a vital role in building protests over president Viktor Yanukovych's refusal to partner with the European Union on November 21, 2013. Angry citizens demanded that he resign. Journalist Mustafa Nayyem recalls his actions that night: "Around 8:00 p.m., I posted on Facebook: 'Come on guys, let's be serious. If you really want to do something, don't just "like" this post. Write that you are ready, and we can try to start something.' Within an hour, there were more than 600 comments."[11] When he suggested demonstrating in the capital at 10:30 p.m., one thousand citizens showed up.

Over the next three months, protesters called for an election to replace the president—and implored their friends to join. The campaign came to be known as Euromaydan (or Euromaidan). Its Facebook page drew more than 125,000 followers in its first two weeks and eventually hit 300,000. Through social media, the group organized, shared photos when soldiers killed dissenters, and for perhaps the first time ever on social media, negotiated demands. In January the president offered opposition leader Arseniy Yatsenyuk a position as prime minister if he would end the revolt. Yatsenyuk tweeted directly to the president that there would be "no deal. . . . The people decide our leaders, not you."[12] By late February almost 11 million tweets had been sent about the movement—and the ousted president had fled. Experts at the Social Media and Political Participation laboratory concluded, "The Ukrainian Euromaidan protest movement may go down in history as the first truly successful social media uprising."[13]

> "The Ukrainian Euromaidan protest movement may go down in history as the first truly successful social media uprising."[13]
>
> —The Social Media and Political Participation laboratory

16

Social Campaigns and Crowdfunding

Similarly, social networking can raise awareness and money for social causes. Younger people in particular are posting about causes they care about; 61 percent of people aged sixteen to thirty-six who were polled by CauseVox in 2016 had done so in the previous week. People also use social media for crowdfunding, raising money by collecting small donations from lots of people through sites like Kickstarter.

Consider this example: In 2017 a women's rights march drew 5 million participants on all seven continents and became the biggest day of demonstrations in US history. The marchers were protesting the presidential inauguration of Donald Trump, whose policies they saw as hostile to women. Four females who organized the event said they did so to "send a bold message to our new ad-

> "It isn't the same kind of networking that happens at conventions, where you're . . . awkwardly attempting to make small talk. LinkedIn is networking without the pressure."[15]
>
> —Technology writer Melanie Pinola

ministration on their first day in office, and to the world[,] that women's rights are human rights."[14] Having publicized and organized the march via social media, the group surpassed its goal of $2 million in less than two months. After the event, women said it inspired them to run for public office—by April 2017 more than twelve times as many women were interested as in the previous year, proving that the march had great impact.

Better Employment Options

For both job applicants and recruiters, social networking is an important tool. Sites like LinkedIn allow job seekers to advertise themselves and to research companies in which mutual connections work. Technology writer Melanie Pinola points out, "One of the great things about LinkedIn is it isn't the same kind of networking that happens at conventions, where you're wearing a name tag, trying to meet strangers, and awkwardly attempting to make small talk. LinkedIn is networking without the pressure."[15]

For companies, the vast majority—92 percent—utilize social media when hiring, according to a 2015 survey. Many employers review applicants' profiles to learn more about them than what an interview can reveal. Malcolm Cox, a director at the advertising technology company Grapeshot, explains what resulted when he interviewed a manager he called Lizzie. He recalls, "While she looked great on paper and was quite endearing in person, we got the sense that she was hiding her true essence. She claimed to lead a boring, quiet life." When he checked her Twitter feed, he discovered that "on weekends, Lizzie transformed herself with the help of face paint into an alter ego, 'Catface,' a feline rave denizen. . . . We offered her a job on the spot."[16] His company appreciated her creativity. Like Cox, almost 40 percent of recruiters have determined via social media that a candidate's personality would mesh with their company.

Leveling the Playing Field

Social networking provides a platform for people to promote themselves and ultimately achieve equality. Historically, women have been at a disadvantage compared to men in launching their careers, for instance. Female entrepreneurs typically start their businesses with half as much money as men do, as well as with fewer professional contacts. Yet through social media, women are networking, sharing advice, hosting Twitter chats with experts, and crowdfunding so well that career expert Geri Stengel says, "Impressively, women raise more than men both in terms of the number of contributions and the amount."[17] The number of female entrepreneurs is growing at twice the rate of males—and by 2030 women could control two-thirds of America's wealth, providing another example of social networking's benefits to society.

Social Networking Harms Society

"People need to take a step back from social media and realize what it is doing to [the millennial] generation. We are a generation obsessed with technology and social media and it is harming the well-being of our population."

—Savina Patheja, a biomedical sciences student

Savina Patheja, "5 Reasons Social Media Is Destroying Our Generation," Odyssey, May 2, 2016. www.theodysseyonline.com.

Consider these questions as you read:

1. How does the claim that there is big money in publishing fake news support the argument that fake news is rampant on social media? Do you find this persuasive? Explain.

2. In your opinion, how convincing is the argument that social networking has caused people to have shorter attention spans? Which facts or examples are the strongest, and why?

3. Do you believe that social media sites like Facebook help expose people to a greater range of ideas or that they promote closed-mindedness? Explain your answer.

Editor's note: The discussion that follows presents common arguments made in support of this perspective, reinforced by facts, quotes, and examples taken from various sources.

Though social networking is sometimes praised for its ability to disseminate useful information, its risks to society greatly outweigh any perceived benefits. Science writer Lucy Goodchild van Hilten asserts that social media is a format "where information is not vetted and people can jump to conclusions quickly."[18] In addition to promoting the spread of potentially dangerous misinformation and prejudiced beliefs, social media is detrimental to people's attention spans and critical-thinking skills.

Hoaxes and Fake News

Perhaps the most alarming aspect of social networking is that hoaxes and fake stories are not only rampant, they are just as likely to go viral as real stories are. That is the summary of research conducted by computer scientist Filippo Menczer, who warns, "If you get your news from social media, as most Americans do, you are exposed to a daily dose of hoaxes, rumors, conspiracy theories and misleading news. When it's all mixed in with reliable information from honest sources, the truth can be very hard to discern."[19] Unfortunately, there's big money in fake news. In 2017 the news show *60 Minutes* interviewed a man who made more than $10,000 a month publishing salacious articles from which he earned money from advertisers for every story read. One of his stories claimed the US Army quarantined a town in Texas that had an Ebola outbreak—all lies, yet it garnered 8 million page views. The views are partly from people who are fooled by the stories, but also by scammers who employ computer software called bots. Bots are fake social networking accounts that automatically "like" or share certain posts to make it appear as though they have been read thousands of times, giving them legitimacy.

> "If you get your news from social media, as most Americans do, you are exposed to a daily dose of hoaxes, rumors, conspiracy theories and misleading news."[19]
>
> —Filippo Menczer, professor of informatics and computer science at Indiana University–Bloomington

Most concerning, fake news can have dire consequences. It had the potential to start a public panic over the Ebola story, for example. In one case, a conspiracy theory circulated that a Washington, DC, pizzeria was operating a child sex trafficking ring. James Alefantis, the owner of the business, lamented, "It went from a few people buzzing about something online or inside of chat rooms that we never would have seen before, to suddenly being blasted to millions and millions of people."[20] Not only did he receive death threats, but a gunman stormed the pizzeria and fired an assault rifle in an attempt to rescue the children. Fortunately, no one was injured. And, equally important, no evidence of child slavery was found.

Although defenders of social networking claim that Google and Facebook now have policies to prevent publishers from making money off fake news stories, these do not go far enough. The policies govern only advertising but do nothing to quell the fake stories themselves. As writers for the *New York Times* point out, "Facebook's ad policy update will not stem the flow of fake news stories that spread through the news feeds that people see when they visit the social network."[21]

Short Attention Spans and the Myth of Multitasking

A particularly harmful aspect of social networking sites is that they offer multiple actions simultaneously, requiring users to divide attention between a real-time updated home screen, chat, status updates, videos, and more. The problem is humans are unable to multitask well. In fact, psychiatrist Edward M. Hallowell defines multitasking as "a mythical activity in which people believe they can perform two or more tasks simultaneously."[22]

Research indicates that people who heavily multitask media are barely able to filter out distractions and do poorly when tested on their ability to switch tasks. What is more, the quality and depth of a person's thought are degraded as more tasks are added. One social media user grieves, "I used to really take the time to digest content. I would read longer paragraphs online and thoroughly enjoy it. But now, I only read lists online. The clutter and barrage of noise has led me to only consume bullet point information."[23] As a result of social networking, people are developing permanently shorter attention spans, which is defined as the time one can concentrate on a task without being distracted. In 2015 a Microsoft survey of Canadians found that the average attention span is only eight seconds. That is four seconds less than it was fifteen years earlier—and, according to biologists, is shorter than that of a fly.

Costly and Dangerous Distractions

During meals, at the movies, at work, pretty much in any place that has an Internet connection—people are distracted and wasting time on

Social Media Provides a Platform for Spreading Hate

Social media provides a venue for hate and prejudice to flourish. Indeed, hate group activity online has increased in recent years, according to Safe Home, a company that conducts and shares research to promote home security. When it studied the Twitter accounts of hate groups, for example, it found that a shocking number of them have amassed thousands of followers to whom they spread their messages of hate.

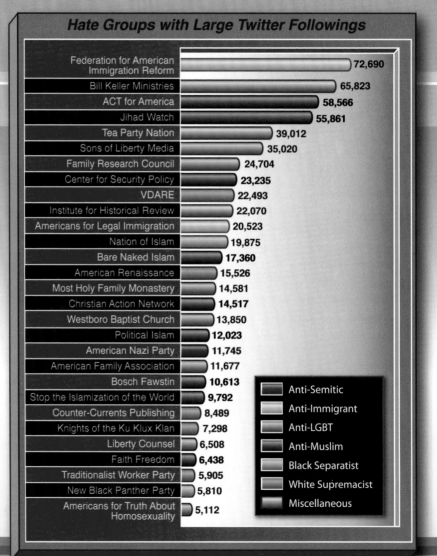

Hate Groups with Large Twitter Followings

Federation for American Immigration Reform	72,690
Bill Keller Ministries	65,823
ACT for America	58,566
Jihad Watch	55,861
Tea Party Nation	39,012
Sons of Liberty Media	35,020
Family Research Council	24,704
Center for Security Policy	23,235
VDARE	22,493
Institute for Historical Review	22,070
Americans for Legal Immigration	20,523
Nation of Islam	19,875
Bare Naked Islam	17,360
American Renaissance	15,526
Most Holy Family Monastery	14,581
Christian Action Network	14,517
Westboro Baptist Church	13,850
Political Islam	12,023
American Nazi Party	11,745
American Family Association	11,677
Bosch Fawstin	10,613
Stop the Islamization of the World	9,792
Counter-Currents Publishing	8,489
Knights of the Ku Klux Klan	7,298
Liberty Counsel	6,508
Faith Freedom	6,438
Traditionalist Worker Party	5,905
New Black Panther Party	5,810
Americans for Truth About Homosexuality	5,112

Legend:
- Anti-Semitic
- Anti-Immigrant
- Anti-LGBT
- Anti-Muslim
- Black Separatist
- White Supremacist
- Miscellaneous

Source: Safe Home, "Hate on Social Media: A Look at Hate Groups and Their Twitter Presence," 2016. www.safehome.org.

social media. Matt Cutts, a former Google software engineer, points out how easily people become absorbed with social networking. He says jokingly, "When you've got 5 minutes to fill, Twitter is a great way to fill 35 minutes."[24] Productivity in the workplace is destroyed, too. For example, three in five people have used social media at work, costing companies trillions of dollars in lost productivity. And they are not logging in for just a few minutes. A 2016 study by TeamLease, an employment services company in India, found that workers spend an average of 2.35 hours per day accessing personal social media accounts, causing work productivity to drop by 13 percent.

More dangerously, pedestrians and drivers have been hurt because they were distracted by social media on their phones. Three teenaged girls died in 2011 while taking a selfie on train tracks as a train whizzed by, not realizing that another train was behind them. A huge number of people use social media while driving, as shocking as that is. Research by the media company AT&T discovered that about four in ten smartphone users do so. Despina Stavrinos, director of an injury-prevention laboratory in Alabama, warns that a driver writing a social media message looks away from the road for five seconds at a time, which, unsurprisingly, significantly increases the risk of crashing.

Closed-Mindedness and Bias

While some people praise social networking for presenting diverse viewpoints, it is more often to blame for perpetuating bias and racism. Social media sites' filters show users the same types of posts that they or their friends have "liked." Consequently, people see posts that reinforce their views, and they are not shown contrary beliefs. Research indicates that Facebook users are likely to passively accept viewpoints and even racist messages shared by friends. Digital content specialist Bindi Donnelly explains, "The very structure of Facebook is one that promotes complicity: we 'Like,' share and affirm. . . . Facebook's affirmative culture, repetitive presentation of messages, and . . . mob mentality may have the suggestive power to steer our thoughts down an undesirable path."[25]

Indeed, hate groups—which demonize people based on their race, gender, sexual orientation, or religion—have seen increased activity on social media. From 2014 to 2015 the number of "likes" on hate group tweets and comments tripled, and from 2015 to 2016 they tripled again. Members of these groups, just like most other groups on social media, primarily share posts that reinforce their own beliefs. Anti-immigrant hate groups, for example, post messages that immigrants commit more crimes than US natives do, yet their members likely do not hear that this claim has been proved false by the Cato Institute, the Sentencing Project, and other respected organizations.

A Shallow Society

In effect, social networking is dumbing down society. Ronald Alsop, author of *The Trophy Kids Grow Up*, a book about millennial employees, endorses this view when he says, "The need for round-the-clock connection not only makes people more impatient, it also robs them of time for quiet reflection or deeper, more critical thinking."[26] Studies seem to support that the more computers and the Internet are incorporated into daily life, the more degraded are people's abilities to analyze and think critically. A society of people with thoughts no more complex than 140-character messages on Twitter is hardly an intelligent one. Everyone can benefit from being better informed, better able to concentrate, and less distracted by social networking.

Chapter Two

Does Social Networking Weaken People's Social Skills?

Social Networking Hinders Social Interactions

- Because people often present a false and overly positive version of themselves on social media, friendships tend to be superficial.
- Distracted by social networking, people neglect their real-life relationships.
- Social network users experience isolation, social anxiety, and depression.
- Social networking is destroying people's communication skills.

The Debate at a Glance

Social Networking Improves Social Interactions

- Through social networking, it is easy for people, even shy ones, to meet others who share their interests.
- Social networking is helping people maintain deeper, more meaningful relationships.
- Those who suffer from depression and anxiety have credited social networking with aiding in their recovery.
- Social networking is changing communication by making people more honest and willing to break social stigmas.

Social Networking Hinders Social Interactions

"I used to care more about real, tangible things—like my relationships with others. Now I find that being watered down with cares about a virtual world—how my image looks on social media or how many 'likes' my instagram photo got."

— Online marketing consultant Neal Samudre

Neal Samudre, "8 Dangers of Social Media We're Not Willing to Admit," *Relevant*, April 19, 2016. www.relevantmagazine.com.

Consider these questions as you read:

1. How persuasive is the argument that social media friendships are more shallow than real-world ones? Provide evidence from the following discussion or your own experience.
2. Can you describe a time that you or someone around you was distracted by social media? What effect did it have on the interaction, on you, and on the people around you?
3. In which situations do you prefer communicating through social media, and which situations are better in person? Why?

Editor's note: The discussion that follows presents common arguments made in support of this perspective, reinforced by facts, quotes, and examples taken from various sources.

Although social networking allows people to amass lots of connections, these friendships are superficial. That is because most social networkers present a fake, edited version of themselves. According to a British survey in 2015 by the cell phone company HTC, more than 75 percent of users post images to make their lives seem more exciting. What is more, it is easy for people to crop something unattractive from a photo, decide *not* to write a post admitting their mistakes, or untag themselves from embarrassing posts. "Essentially, we are all professionals at making reality look like an elaborate photo story of the sheer perfection that composes our lives. But it isn't real. . . . We aren't the people we pretend to be online,"[27] asserts Lexi Herrick, a digital marketer.

Superficial Friendships

When relationships are based on the fake image people present—rather than on people truly getting to know each other—they are shallow. In fact, many people think their social network friendships are more meaningful than they are. Jay Baer, president of a marketing strategy firm, argues, "Social media forces upon us a feeling of intimacy and closeness that doesn't actually exist." He describes two people he connected with via social networking and worked closely with for years, yet one has never been to his home, and the other has a daughter he has never met. "I consider these people (and many, many others) to be friends, and I'm thankful that social media has brought them into my life. But in comparison to my pre-social media friends (many of whom I've known for 30+ years), I know almost nothing about them."[28] He, like many who are cynical of social networking, questions that people are spending time on shallow online relationships when they could be building more valuable offline ones.

> "We aren't the people we pretend to be online."[27]
>
> —Lexi Herrick, a digital marketer and founder of the website Her Track

Even the definition of *friend* itself has been devalued by social networking. Now people consider *friend* to mean those they are only loosely connected to, such as former classmates or coworkers, and even people they have never met. In support of this view, Oxford University professor Robin Dunbar found that the average Facebook user has 150 friends, but only 15 could be considered actual friends, and only 5 are close friends. She declares, "Real (as opposed to casual) relationships require at least occasional face-to-face interaction to maintain them,"[29] suggesting that the majority of Facebook friends are only casual acquaintances.

Social Networking Hurts People's Social Skills

When adults were asked how social networking impacts their lives, many reported that it has negative effects on their relationships and self-esteem. The vast majority also said that social media allows people to easily deceive others. These are the findings of behavioral scientist Clarissa Silva, who conducted in-depth interviews with social media users between the ages of twenty-eight and seventy-three.

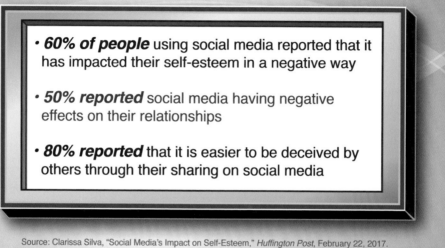

- **60% of people** using social media reported that it has impacted their self-esteem in a negative way

- **50% reported** social media having negative effects on their relationships

- **80% reported** that it is easier to be deceived by others through their sharing on social media

Source: Clarissa Silva, "Social Media's Impact on Self-Esteem," *Huffington Post*, February 22, 2017. www.huffingtonpost.com.

Disconnected and Never Present

No matter where they are or what they are doing, many people are often distracted by social networking. Because it is available on their cell phones, they are constantly connected to it. Ann Smarty, a manager at the company Internet Marketing Ninjas, complains, "I *hate* being out in public and seeing people on their phones. . . . Whether it is grocery shopping, getting dinner with friends or waiting in line, it is just so impolite. It also shows a serious problem with distraction in today's society. We can't enjoy the world around us for an hour without retreating back into that safe little digital box."[30] Polls show that 22 percent of Americans check their social networking accounts multiple times a day, and 55 percent of Facebook users do so.

These numbers indicate that social media users are never fully focused on the present or the people around them. Behrouz Jafarnezhad, a digital marketing consultant and PhD researcher, explains the dichotomy this way: "What's supposed to connect people and make them more 'social,' disconnects them from real people—and connects them to real virtual people."[31] While he endorses connecting with people online, he does not think this should happen at the cost of friends and family, whom people ignore because they are social networking. The practice has become so common that it has been nicknamed "phubbing," short for "phone-snubbing," or paying attention to one's own phone instead of the other person. In Jafarnezhad's observation, some parents scold their kids for being distracted by social networking, "but the same parents usually have one eye on their smartphones, doing email or social media, at breakfast while their kids are talking to them."[32]

Prone to Isolation and Depression

Despite claims that social networking helps people feel connected to others, the data actually reveal that people who spend more time on social networking sites feel *more* socially isolated and unhappy. Research published in *American Journal of Preventive Medicine* in 2017 found that of people aged nineteen to thirty-two, those who used social networking for more than two hours each day were twice as likely to feel socially isolated than those who used it for less than a half hour a day. Social media use made them less likely to feel a sense of belonging or have fulfilling relationships. Brian Primack, professor of pediatrics and the lead study author, opines, "We are inherently social creatures, but modern life tends to compartmentalize us instead of bringing us together. While it may seem that social media presents opportunities to fill that social void, I think this study suggests that it may not be the solution."[33]

> "What's supposed to connect people and make them more 'social,' disconnects them from real people."[31]
>
> —Behrouz Jafarnezhad, a digital marketing consultant and PhD researcher

29

It is not just isolation that social media users feel; some feel depressed as well. In Primack's study, participants who reported using the most social media platforms (seven to eleven) had more than three times the risk of depression and anxiety than those who used zero to two platforms. One way in which social networking can trigger depression is people are likely to compare themselves to their friends' lives as seen on their social media and feel unhappy with their own life as a result. Kelsey, a sophomore at Ohio State University, asserts, "If I'm already having a bad day or feeling especially self-conscious, scrolling through my News Feed can actually make me feel incredibly depressed."[34] Indeed, one in five people surveyed in the United Kingdom blame social media for making them feel depressed when they see friends post about their lives. While people tend to feel that their interactions with online friends count as socializing, these friendships pose special problems that demonstrate there is no substitute for real-life relationships.

Destroying Communication Skills

A common complaint is that social skills are deteriorating as more people use short messages and emojis to communicate instead of conversations. Sending a message through social networking is impersonal and does not compare to real conversation. "Voice inflection, body language, facial expression and the [chemical] pheromones (released during face-to-face interaction): These are all fundamental to establishing human relationships. And they're all missing with most forms of modern technology,"[35] contends psychologist Jim Taylor.

As social media is becoming a preferred method of communication, young people are not mastering social skills they need. Catholic Bible study leader Jay Hauck laments, "All the time spent on social media can harm a child's ability to have real, in-person conversations. It's amazing to see teens at a restaurant where they're all on their phones and not one is talking to another."[36] Nor are young people developing the communication skills to navigate in the working world. According to experts in adolescent development, many young adults do not know how to conduct themselves in job interviews, collaborate with team members or clients, or react appropriately to criticism. It has become such a problem that 60 percent of employers surveyed in 2016 said that job candidates' social skills are more important than their IQ.

Petty Interactions

Almost everyone who has used social networking has found themselves in a tiff with a friend over a comment that was misunderstood or sparked jealousy. Sonoma State University student Emily Alampi agrees that social media causes her, like many other people, to get worked up over "silly" things. She suggests taking a break from it: "I give myself anxiety over what I see on Facebook and it's truly unhealthy for me, as well as my relationship. After spending time away . . . , I've found that I have a much stronger relationship with my boyfriend because I'm not worrying over problems that actually don't exist."[37] As examples like this demonstrate, the effects of social networking on relationships are, on the whole, negative.

Social Networking Improves Social Interactions

"Social media provides the opportunity to have and be a friend, to congregate without leaving the house, to never be alone."

—Barry Birkett, technology expert

Barry Birkett, "5 Benefits of Social Media for Seniors—Let's Help Them Get Online!," Senior Care Corner. www.seniorcarecorner.com.

Consider these questions as you read:

1. Taking into account the points made in this discussion, would you rather meet new people through social networking or in person? Why?
2. What is meant by the assertion that social media is changing communication? Is this positive or negative, in your opinion? Support your answer.
3. When people use social media, how honest do you think they are about their lives—and does this matter? Explain.

Editor's note: The discussion that follows presents common arguments made in support of this perspective, reinforced by facts, quotes, and examples taken from various sources.

Through social networking, users gain access to billions of people around the world, providing countless opportunities to make new friends, strengthen existing relationships, and get emotional support. Indeed, 52 percent of teenagers claim that social media has a positive impact on their friendships, while only 4 percent view its impact as negative. Moreover, contrary to what many people think, social media is actually getting people to communicate more openly and honestly.

New Friends with Shared Interests

A major benefit of social networking is that it is easier for people to meet others online than face-to-face. Benjamin Wareing, a seventeen-year-old in Britain, contends, "Social media is a great way to make new friends with similar interests to mine." Interested in both politics and journalism, he conducted an experiment on social media. He explains the aftermath: "I became a viral hit, being picked up by *The New York Times*. From that moment, lots of Americans added me and we still talk to this day about politics. The likes of Twitter and Facebook have given me a chance to make friends all over the world."[38] Like Wareing, 64 percent of teens aged thirteen to seventeen who have made a new friend online did so through social networking, which provides a way to quickly find people with shared interests. From groups devoted to even the rarest of hobbies to gaming social networks with thousands of users, there is a circle of friends for everyone.

Furthermore, people who are shy report that social media makes it easier for them to socialize. Novel writer Adelle Waldman points out, "Social media seems to be . . . a way to overcome, or at least get around, shyness. I see people who are timid and reserved in person boldly carve out charming (and occasionally not-so-charming) online personalities."[39] People who are nervous during in-person conversations can manage a controlled, comfortable pace through social networking, such as by taking extra time to craft a response or logging out if they get overwhelmed.

Another group that especially benefits from social networking is elderly people, who may be homebound and are prone to loneliness. According to Barry Birkett, whose website provides resources for caregivers of older people, "Seniors are jumping on board Facebook, Twitter, YouTube and more as they realize it is fun and provides real benefits. . . . The importance of socializing as part of a community cannot be overstated, particularly for seniors spending much of their time living isolated at home."[40]

> "Twitter and Facebook have given me a chance to make friends all over the world."[38]
>
> —Benjamin Wareing, age seventeen

Social media allows these people a place to cultivate hobbies, ask questions, learn about activities in their community, and more.

Deep and Meaningful Connection

Despite some claims that social media friendships are shallow, there is evidence that social networking enables people to form deeper ties with friends and family. Statistics produced by the Pew Research Center show that 83 percent of teens who use social networking claim that it keeps them connected to what is happening in their friends' lives, and 70 percent say it keeps them connected to their friends' feelings. Social media can help strengthen emotional ties through updates, chats, or face-to-face technology, especially for people who live far apart. Unlike in the past, no one need pay for international phone calls or wait for letters to arrive. For these reasons, one Yale professor credits social networking for allowing his foreign students to stay in touch with their families, and many grandparents feel much more connected to their grandchildren, too.

Scientific research and testimony from experts bolster the argument that social media can help people forge strong relationships. According to Sofia Kaliarnta, a PhD student studying technology and philosophy, online friendships "can be very personal, deep and meaningful for the individuals concerned, providing companionship, a listening ear in times of need, intellectual discussion and stimulation."[41] Rather than dismissing such friendships as inferior, she recommends focusing on how they can improve people's well-being.

Easing Depression and Anxiety

Although some research has shown that people who spend more time on social networking sites are more prone to depression and anxiety, these studies do not distinguish whether social networking *causes* these ailments or whether people with these problems are simply more likely to spend more time on social networking. In fact, numerous patients have credited social networking with aiding in their mental health recovery. An important part of healing is reconnecting with people, feeling that

People Use Social Networking to Connect With and Support Others

According to a survey of Americans aged sixteen to forty-four, people say they share information on social media to keep their friends apprised of how they feel and what they think, as well as to help support other people in their social networks. The study was conducted by Olapic, a company that helps brands develop content that is visually appealing to consumers.

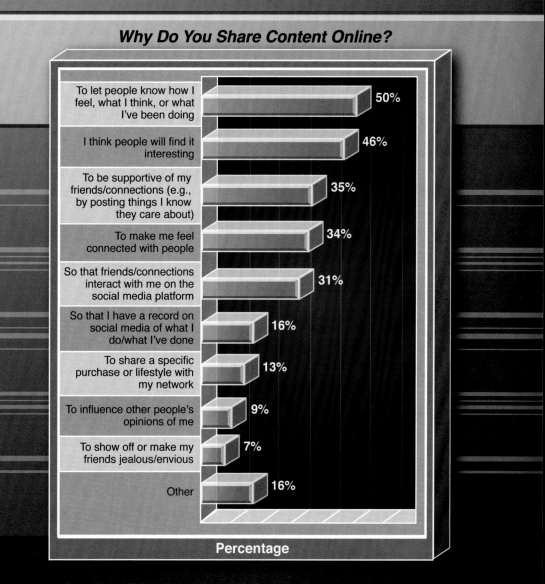

Why Do You Share Content Online?

	Percentage
To let people know how I feel, what I think, or what I've been doing	50%
I think people will find it interesting	46%
To be supportive of my friends/connections (e.g., by posting things I know they care about)	35%
To make me feel connected with people	34%
So that friends/connections interact with me on the social media platform	31%
So that I have a record on social media of what I do/what I've done	16%
To share a specific purchase or lifestyle with my network	13%
To influence other people's opinions of me	9%
To show off or make my friends jealous/envious	7%
Other	16%

Source: Olapic, "US–Olapic Research Report," Morar Consulting, March 23, 2017. www.scribd.com.

they can share without being judged, and getting reassurance that life can improve. Medical doctor Melinda Ring recalls how social networking helped her depressed teenaged son, not only in his recovery but in allowing him to aid others who are struggling. She says that her son, Matthew, "shifted his own Instagram account to be a positive support to others, and he quickly developed more than 6,000 followers, reinforcing that his message of hope and support was needed and appreciated. He also found YouTubers who shared their struggles now and in the past."[42] Then Matthew started his own YouTube channel, and declared in his first video, "I want to be the kind of person that you can say, he helped me through a hard time, and made me smile when I was in a hard place."[43] Ring testifies, "Most clearly what I've heard from my son is about the huge amount of support peers give each other when they are depressed."[44]

Honesty Breaks Stigmas

It is true that social networking is fundamentally changing the way people communicate: People are becoming more honest communicators. Like never before, they are sharing deep thoughts and feelings with large groups. According to communications professor Paul Booth, when people use social networking, they are likely to trust the people with whom they are sharing information, and thus their messages are more honest. Some people do "catfish" others, or pretend to be someone else by setting up a fake profile; however, most people are honest in their profiles because they are linked to friends they know in real life. Dr. Gwendolyn Seidman, author of the social behavior blog *Close Encounters*, reasons that these connections make social media users more honest, because others will call them out if they lie about their age or job, for example. "Surprisingly, people can sometimes be more authentic online than offline," she

> "Your community is a great litmus [test] for both your strengths and weaknesses. I have found that surrounding myself with those I admire, respect and love, I have a network of empowerment."[47]
>
> —Marie Bonaccorse, a social media manager

36

maintains. "If you meet people via Facebook, you're likely to be getting a relatively accurate impression of their overall personality."[45]

All this open communication is leading to another phenomenon. People are more willing to post about their experiences that carry a social stigma, like health problems or divorce. The more people talk about them, the more they are breaking stigmas. On Instagram, for instance, couples have posted final photos together with the #divorceselfie hashtag to show that divorce is not shameful and can be done respectfully. Life coach Nicole Holt says of her divorce selfie that went viral, "I feel like it's my job to inspire people, so I wanted to turn my mess into my message. . . . There are a lot of other people who are . . . going through things that I've gone through, and I wanted people to see that you can be OK."[46]

A Wide Network for Advice and Feedback

Social media allows for open discussion and challenging people's ideas in a constructive way. Marie Bonaccorse, a social media manager who calls herself the Sassy Tweetress, contends, "Your community is a great litmus [test] for both your strengths and weaknesses. I have found that surrounding myself with those I admire, respect and love, I have a network of empowerment. Social media . . . solidifies my philosophies and opinions but keeps me open and accepting for when I need correction."[47] In sum, social networking provides a wider network of friends with whom social networkers can share emotional support and deeply strengthen social ties.

Chapter Three

Is Social Networking Harming Young People?

Social Networking Is Harmful to Young People

- The instant gratification that social networking provides is linked to addiction to social media and lack of patience in young people.
- Using social networking as a youth may lead to low self-esteem and risky behavior such as sexting.
- Social networking can negatively impact learning and development of empathy in young adults.
- Teens are unable to protect themselves from online dangers.

The Debate at a Glance

Social Networking Benefits Young People

- Social networking offers young people praise and support that can boost self-esteem.
- Social networking is helping teens develop a different kind of empathy.
- For students, social networking can foster learning and motivate them to stay in school.
- By protecting their own privacy on social media, teens are learning to be responsible for themselves.

Social Networking Is Harmful to Young People

"Instagram and Snapchat rank . . . as the worst for mental health and wellbeing. Both platforms are very image-focused and it appears that they may be driving feelings of inadequacy and anxiety in young people."

—Shirley Cramer, chief executive of the Royal Society for Public Health

Quoted in Royal Society for Public Health, "Instagram Ranked Worst for Young People's Mental Health," May 19, 2017. www.rsph.org.uk.

Consider these questions as you read:

1. Does the explanation of dopamine's effect on the brain convince you that social networking can harm young people? Why or why not?
2. What reasoning is used for the argument that young people no longer have patience? In your opinion, how convincing is this rationale, and why?
3. How persuasive is the argument that many teens are not addicted to social networking because they take breaks sometimes for a day or even a week? Support your answer using facts or anecdotes.

Editor's note: The discussion that follows presents common arguments made in support of this perspective, reinforced by facts, quotes, and examples taken from various sources.

Because young adults' brains are still developing into their early twenties, they should avoid constant exposure to social media, which can impede their development. The long-term effects of social networking are not fully clear because it is still relatively new, but thus far it has hurt teens' self-esteem, emotional development, and school performance. Therefore, its use must be limited in young people.

Instant Gratification, Addiction, and Impatience

Modern cell phones allow immediate, round-the-clock access to social media. Consequently, young adults are becoming hooked on the instant gratification it provides. Benjamin Gordon, a computer science student, explains: "A typical day for me starts out with me turning off the alarm on my smartphone and immediately taking the opportunity to check all my texts, instant messages, emails, status updates. . . . Every like, every personal message, every post on my feed is a dopamine rush." This "rush" is the effect of chemicals that act on the brain, triggering it to feel good when people receive positive feedback, such as someone retweeting their post. But on the flip side, this gratification is fleeting, and when it wears off, people crave the rush more and more. Gordon describes the rest of his day: "Waiting for a bus—check Facebook. Riding the bus up to campus—I wonder what's on Reddit? Going to the beach—time to send everyone I know a Snapchat!"[48] It is no wonder that young people can become addicted to social media; about 40 percent of people age thirteen to thirty-three admit that they are, according to market researcher Ypulse. Among thirteen-year-olds studied by CNN, some check their accounts one hundred times per day. Mental health experts warn that social media can be just as addictive as drugs in young people—and can have the same adverse effects on the brain and on their lives.

> "Every like, every personal message, every post on my feed is a dopamine rush."[48]
>
> —Benjamin Gordon, a student at the University of California–Santa Cruz

Another problem with instant gratification is people begin to lose a valuable skill: patience. Young people now expect solutions and responses immediately. Author Rachael Tulipano denounces social media for destroying patience. She claims millennials do not respect that "the important milestones in life don't happen overnight. Building a relationship, getting married, earning a successful career, having children and becoming a homeowner. While a large number of 20-somethings feel a rush to reach these landmarks, it's critical to understand these major events take time to develop."[49] After all, she says, these events do not come with instant gratification, yet they do bring joy in life.

Social Media Has Big Negatives for Young Users

Social media is a boon to many young users but also comes with some disturbing negatives. That is the finding of a survey of British social media users ages fourteen to twenty-four. A significant number of Facebook, Snapchat, and Instagram users have experienced negative effects including loss of sleep, poor body image, and fear of missing out on what their friends are experiencing. Participants rated their social media experiences on a scale from -2 (a lot worse), through 0 (no effect), to +2 (a lot better).

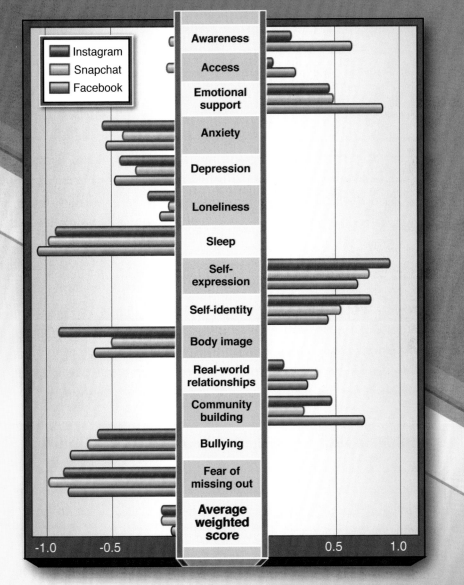

Source: Royal Society for Public Health, "Status of Mind: Social Media and Young People's Mental Health and Wellbeing," 2017. www.rsph.org.uk.

41

Low Self-Esteem and Sexts

On social media, people put their lives on display—but usually only the best parts. When social networkers compare themselves to their friends on social media, they are likely to feel self-conscious or unhappy. For young people, who are still building their confidence, these comparisons can hurt. College student Isla Whately recalls her experience of being a depressed teen: "Social media made me feel worse, as I would constantly compare myself to other people. . . . I'd go on social media, see all my friends doing things and hate myself for not being able to do them, or feel bad that I wasn't as good a person as them."[50]

Girls are even more likely to develop low self-esteem than boys. Complicating matters, they may seek a confidence boost—and "likes"—by posting inappropriate selfies or sexting (sending or receiving sexual content digitally). If youths send a revealing photo, there is a good chance it will one day be shared with someone they did not intend to see it. Psychologist Jennifer Powell-Lunder believes adolescents may be mimicking social media stars such as Kim Kardashian, which is why she posits, "They're really not thinking through the consequences when they put out these pictures. What they're thinking about is that Kim Kardashian put out a [sex] video and now she's one of the most famous people in the entire universe."[51] There is a biological reason young people do not always think rationally—they do not yet have a fully developed prefrontal cortex, the area of the brain that controls impulsivity and helps us make good judgments. Unfortunately, the self-esteem boost from sharing such content on social media quickly wears off, and young people may come to believe that their worth hinges on their appearance and their friends' opinions.

Problems with Learning and Emotional Development

Much of the research on social networking focuses on how it affects child development. Due to the multitasking that social media requires, users are becoming less able to concentrate on a single task. A twenty-three-year-old college student reports how Facebook distracted her and a friend from writing a school paper: "We both procrastinate. . . . The paper was due the next day. We happened to be on Facebook at the same time we were doing this paper, which distracted us the most."[52] This hurt their ability to learn as well as their grades. A 2015 study in the *Journal of Applied Developmental Psychology* found that college freshmen who spent more than two hours a day on Facebook—an hour of that doing schoolwork at the same time—had worse grades than their peers.

Other studies reveal that young people are having trouble developing empathy, the ability to understand what other people are feeling. The more they use social networking instead of in-person communication, the less they are able to identify what emotions are behind other people's words. In fact, a thirty-year study revealed that from 1979 to 2009, empathy decreased by 40 percent among college students due to the rise in computers and decline in face-to-face conversations. Without being able to infer emotions, young people are more likely to say hurtful things. In an interview, comedian Louis C.K. said of young people: "They don't build empathy. Kids are mean, and it's 'cause they're trying it out. They look at a kid and they go, 'You're fat,' and then they see the kid's face scrunch up and they go, 'Ooh, that doesn't feel good to make a person do that.'" Yet when they send the same message from their cell phone, he cautions, they do not see consequences and instead think, "That was fun."[53]

> "I'd go on social media, see all my friends doing things and hate myself for not being able to do them, or feel bad that I wasn't as good a person as them."[50]
>
> —Isla Whately, a college student

Young People Do Not Protect Their Privacy

Of all the risks of social networking, the most dangerous is that young people share too much information. Although experts caution that young social networkers should not disclose their full name or other identifying data, 91 percent of teens post photos of themselves, and eight out of ten list their birth date. This puts them at risk of identity theft or stalking. Making matters worse, most parents do not do enough to protect them or do not know what risks they face; 57 percent of parents surveyed by National Cyber Security Alliance in 2016 disclosed that they are not aware of their kids' online activities. One mother, named Laura, regrets that she let her twelve-year-old daughter open an Instagram account. She admits, "Due to my lack of knowledge (I thought Instagram was basically a glorified camera), I allowed her to have an account. In the last week, she has been indirectly contacted by what appears to be a predatorial pedophile posing as a radio contest to which girls send their photos."[54] Ploys like this are not uncommon. By the time kids are twelve years old, 43 percent of them have messaged with strangers online.

Sadly, that can have severe repercussions. In 2016 thirteen-year-old Nicole Lovell was kidnapped and murdered, allegedly by a man she had met on Kik, a chat app on which teens converse anonymously. "Tragedies like Nicole Lovell's death are fortunately few," says journalist Naomi Schaefer Riley, "but the dangers of social media for our kids are not."[55] The numerous risks that social networking poses for teenagers—including addiction, low self-esteem, and lack of privacy protections—outweigh any benefits it may have.

Social Networking Benefits Young People

"Technology does offer our children positive emotional benefits. Teens are able to connect with their peers more easily through texting and social media, and they feel supported with a variety of networks."

—TeenSafe, a company that helps parents monitor their kids' online activities

TeenSafe, "Do Today's Tech-Obsessed Teens Have Less Empathy?," March 19, 2015. www.teensafe.com.

Consider these questions as you read:

1. Do you believe that using social media boosts or harms self-confidence in teens? Explain your answer.
2. What is meant by "empathy has progressed," and how persuasive is the argument that young people are developing virtual empathy? Explain.
3. Do you think educators should incorporate social media into their classroom instruction? Why or why not?

Editor's note: The discussion that follows presents common arguments made in support of this perspective, reinforced by facts, quotes, and examples taken from various sources.

Through social networking, young people get some of the social interaction and support they need for proper emotional development. According to a survey published in 2017 by the Associated Press and the University of Chicago, 78 percent of teens say they use social media to stay connected to their friends, and 42 percent to connect with family. This technology is helping young people feel confident, compassionate, and engaged in their school. But it is not making them addicted to it, as some cynics charge. The same poll revealed that 58 percent of thirteen- to seventeen-year-olds who use social media have taken at least one break away from it, and half of them logged out for a week or more. Used in moderation, social networking is a powerful tool.

Feeling Encouraged and Empowered

In a poll by Common Sense Media, one in five teens responded that social media makes them feel more confident. Many young adults get encouraging messages from their networks. For instance, when a site called KidzVuz helped promote the Tony Awards for Broadway productions, kids were asked to post videos of themselves singing songs from musicals or sharing why they love theater. The cofounder of KidzVuz, Rebecca Levey, summarizes its success: "The response from other kids was so awesome. I mean we had kids who were truly tone deaf and it didn't matter. Everyone's like, 'You're awesome,' 'Go follow your dream,' 'Don't give up.'"[56]

Selfies, which are especially popular with young people, may have bonus benefits. While Eileen Masio, mother of two, admits that social networking can be damaging, she claims it can "help to build self-confidence, too. When [my kids] post selfies, all the comments I usually see are 'You're beautiful,' 'You're so pretty,' 'Oh my God, gorgeous.'"[57] According to a 2014 survey, 65 percent of teenaged girls credited seeing their selfie photos on social media with boosting their confidence. That may be because selfies actually feature two aspects of the person posting them. Pamela Rutledge, director of the Media Psychology Research Center, points out: "It's the first time you get to be the photographer *and* the subject of the photograph. Even though that seems very simple, that's an extraordinary shift, historically. And control makes people believe in themselves."[58] Hence, a "like" on a selfie is praising someone twice, as both a model and as a photographer.

> "When [my kids] post selfies, all the comments I usually see are 'You're beautiful,' 'You're so pretty,' 'Oh my God, gorgeous.'"[57]
>
> —Eileen Masio of New York

Teens Say Social Networking Makes Them Feel More Connected and Informed

The Associated Press–NORC Center for Public Affairs Research at the University of Chicago conducted a study of the social media habits of teenagers, ages thirteen to seventeen. It found that a large number of teens feel more connected to their friends and family through social networking, and many also feel better informed. Nearly one in five report that they feel supported because of their social networks. All of these statistics indicate that social media offers many advantages for young people.

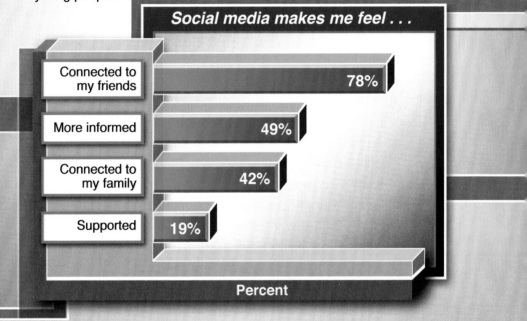

Source: The Associated Press–NORC Center for Public Affairs Research, "American Teens Are Taking Breaks from Social Media; Some Step Back Deliberately, but Other Breaks Are Involuntary," April 2017. www.apnorc.org.

Not only does positive feedback make young adults feel empowered, it actually causes changes in the brain that give them a boost. Supporting this argument, a team at the University of California–Los Angeles studied teenagers' brains while the teens saw that they received "likes" on social media. The reward center of the brain was triggered, releasing chemicals that make a person feel good. Lead author Lauren Sherman observes, "When teens learn that their own pictures have supposedly received a lot of likes, they show significantly greater activation in parts of the brain's reward circuitry. This is the same group of regions responding when we see pictures of a person we love or when we win money."[59]

Virtual Empathy Becomes Real Empathy

Some critics of social networking charge that the rise of virtual communication is hindering young people's development of empathy, or the ability to understand someone else's emotions. However, empathy is not disappearing, it is merely changing. For example, during conversation, people mimic each other's facial expressions to relay compassion, but that is not possible on social networking platforms. Instead, people began showing empathy through emoticons—faces made from text characters, such as :'(for crying. As technology improved, they used emojis and stickers, which are pictures that communicate emotions and phrases. In a 2015 poll, the marketing company Emogi discovered that 92 percent of people on the Internet use emojis and that they do so to express what they are thinking and to promote understanding.

Another way social media friends convey compassion is by "liking" or commenting on status updates. Research published in the journal *Computers in Human Behavior* in 2015 examined the relationship between young people's Internet use, their empathy online ("virtual empathy"), and face-to-face (real-world) empathy. When people spent more time online, they did not have less real-world empathy. Moreover, the more time that youths spent social networking, the better able they were to express empathy online, and those who expressed it were more likely to offer it in the real world. One of the study's authors, Larry D. Rosen, posits that empathy has progressed as technology has. He emphasizes that young people today are more compassionate toward people who are different—homosexual

> "If you need empathy and kindness you can find it on Facebook and other social media. It may not be as good as in real life, but it counts."[60]
>
> —Larry D. Rosen, a research psychologist, educator, and author of a study on empathy

or transgender, for instance—because they are more exposed to different people via social media. Rosen concludes, "If you need empathy and kindness you can find it on Facebook and other social media. It may not be as good as in real life, but it counts because it makes you feel better."[60]

Improved School Performance

Among students, social networking can help improve writing skills, school engagement, and high school graduation rates. English teacher Rusul Alrubail suggests that it be used to inspire students to write and express their voice. She proposes, "We need to help students see that their blogging, texting, tweeting on social media is real writing. *Their writing is real writing because their writing is their voice.* Student voice needs to be nurtured and appreciated in the classroom, regardless the outlet they use to communicate it."[61]

In many schools, educators incorporate sites like Facebook into their instruction; others use sites designed specifically for their school. Whatever network is used, social media can keep students engaged and less likely to drop out. That is because it is easy for pupils to get assignments or links from their teacher's page, ask questions, and engage in discussion through online posts. Walden University doctoral student Rebecca Mix Yard conducted a study that revealed students are more motivated to stay in school when they can use social media to access class materials and communicate with teachers. She concludes, "Social media is a ubiquitous part of our society. Harnessing its potential to create positive influences on student learning goals could provide the impetus for school success and increase high school graduation rates."[62]

Teens Exert Control over Their Privacy

Though some worried adults wish to heavily restrict young people's social media use, experts recommend that they should instead empower youngsters to protect their privacy. But in fact, evidence shows that young adults already skillfully monitor their privacy settings, limit the audience who can see each post, or use aliases on profiles. When a small group of students at Santa Clara University were polled in 2016, an astounding 92 percent responded that they have adjusted their social media privacy settings, and 42 percent eschewed certain platforms that do not offer enough privacy protections. Young people's desire to keep the content of their messages private is evidenced by the rise of networks like Snapchat that delete messages as soon as they are seen by both parties. Of Snapchat's 166 million users, the majority are under twenty-five years old. All of this suggests that teens are taking responsibility for protecting themselves online.

Moreover, many young people are better versed in privacy settings than most adults are. Jacqui Cheng, who taught a six-week technology course to high school students, was surprised by what they taught *her*. She maintains, "These teenagers were extremely savvy with privacy on social media, sometimes to the point of bafflement. For example, did you know that many teens 'delete' their Facebook accounts altogether every time the rest of us would just log out?" Their profiles reappear the next time they log in, but this allows them "to stay under the radar from nosy friend, parent, or public searches while they're not online."[63]

In sum, not only do most young people use social networking in a way that protects their privacy, but they clearly are supporting each other and thriving in many other ways on social media. And as the next generations are raised in a world with social networking, one that is more technologically connected than anyone in the past experienced, social media's benefits will continue to grow even greater than its creators could have imagined.

Chapter Four

Does Social Networking Facilitate Crime and Violence?

Social Networking Helps Solve Crimes and Prevent Violence

- Shared social media posts help identify and locate kidnapped children.
- Social networks help police identify and track down criminals.
- Some wrongdoers incriminate themselves via social networking.
- Through social networking, suicides and school shootings have been prevented.

The Debate at a Glance

Social Networking Fuels Crime and Violence

- Cyberbullying via social networking is becoming common and provides constant access to the victim.
- Privacy-violating practices lead to stalking, burglary, and stolen identities.
- Social networking is a haven for sexual predators.
- Hate crimes are on the rise due to social networking hate groups.

Social Networking Helps Solve Crimes and Prevent Violence

"Cops can use social media sites to gather valuable intelligence on suspected criminals. Not only can police use social media to solve crimes, but they can also use it to help find missing, endangered or distressed people."

—Timothy Roufa, a Florida police officer

Timothy Roufa, "The Use of Social Networking in Law Enforcement," Balance, April 17, 2017. www.thebalance.com.

Consider these questions as you read:

1. Do you think that law enforcement officials should be given greater access to people's private social networking profiles, and if so, under what circumstances? Explain your answer.
2. Do you believe broadcasting details of crimes is a good use of social networks? Why or why not?
3. What are the benefits and pitfalls of citizens taking photos of suspicious individuals and license plates and distributing them on social media?

Editor's note: The discussion that follows presents common arguments made in support of this perspective, reinforced by facts, quotes, and examples taken from various sources.

Social networking is an important tool in investigating crime, according to 82 percent of law enforcement officials polled by the research company LexisNexis. While an investigator generally cannot view information that people have set as private, sometimes their social media friends will offer access to private messages or posts visible only to friends. Agents may also pose as someone else to ensnare a suspect. In rare cases of immediate danger, a social media site may grant authorities access to a member's account. Moreover, social networkers themselves are helping fight crime. According to the National Crime Prevention Council, "One tweet to your neighbors about a strange person peering into a neighbor's house in the area or a post on Facebook about an attempted child abduction can instantly put hundreds of your neighbors on alert and get them all working together to help law enforcement apprehend the suspects."[64] In all of these ways, social networking is proving uniquely useful in gathering data on victims and suspects, locating evidence, and even preventing tragedies.

Publicizing and Rescuing Kidnapped Children

Possibly the first use of social networking to broadcast a missing child was in 2007, for Madeleine McCann, a three-year-old who disappeared in Portugal. "Within minutes of her going missing, relatives were able to send high-quality video of her—posting them on websites, Facebook pages and sending them to news desks,"[65] maintains her family's spokesperson, Clarence Mitchell. Sadly, Madeleine has not been found, but through social networking, awareness of her case increased over the years—and so has social media's role in fighting crime.

The AMBER Alert system was developed to broadcast details about abducted children and the suspects through TV and radio bulletins. Citizens began sharing this information on social media, spreading awareness and helping locate victims. One example was shared by Facebook cofounder Mark Zuckerberg, who posted a photo captioned, "Baby Victoria, who was abducted last year [2014] from a hospital in Trois Rivières, Québec, and safely returned to her parents after someone in our community saw an alert on Facebook."[66] Inspired by stories like this, Facebook partnered

> "Within minutes of her going missing, relatives were able to send high-quality video of her—posting them on websites, Facebook pages and sending them to news desks."[65]
>
> —Clarence Mitchell, spokesperson for the family of missing girl Madeleine McCann

Social Networking Helps Fight Crimes

The International Association of Chiefs of Police and the Urban Institute conducted a poll of law enforcement agencies about their use of social media. Most reported that it is a valuable tool in keeping the public apprised of safety concerns, soliciting crime tips, and investigating crime.

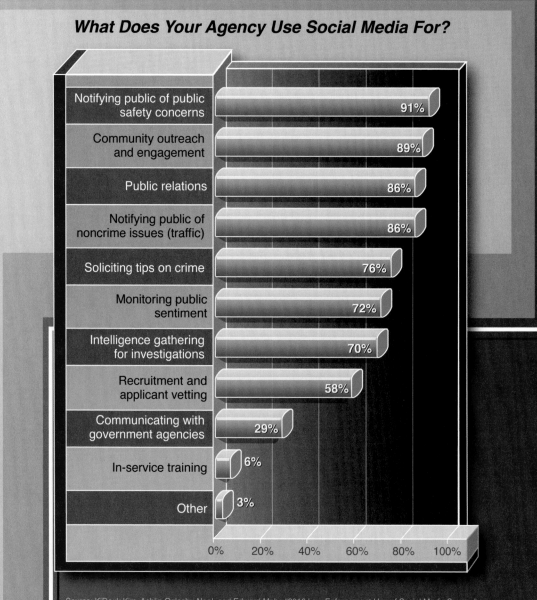

What Does Your Agency Use Social Media For?

Category	Percentage
Notifying public of public safety concerns	91%
Community outreach and engagement	89%
Public relations	86%
Notifying public of noncrime issues (traffic)	86%
Soliciting tips on crime	76%
Monitoring public sentiment	72%
Intelligence gathering for investigations	70%
Recruitment and applicant vetting	58%
Communicating with government agencies	29%
In-service training	6%
Other	3%

Source: KiDeuk Kim, Ashlin Oglesby-Neal, and Edward Mohr, "2016 Law Enforcement Use of Social Media Survey," International Association of Chiefs of Police and the Urban Institute, February 2017. www.theiacp.org.

with the National Center for Missing & Exploited Children in 2015 to display AMBER Alerts on its news feed to give the alerts the most visibility and save even more lives.

Targeting Criminals

In the past, authorities posted illustrations of criminals in communal areas for months or years before someone recognized them. Today, in a fraction of the time, social networking users can help identify unknown suspects and locate known criminals. In one case, social media user Nick Hedges saw a police photo of his Facebook friend robbing a gas station. After turning him in, Hedges said he "definitely felt obligated to do it, and somebody doing that, they shouldn't be running the streets."[67]

The public can help police find criminals in other ways, too. For example, two gay men were savagely attacked on a street in Philadelphia in 2014, and the suspects were captured on camera. Quickly, the social networking community worked together to identify the attackers. One user found a publicly posted group photo from that night that showed people dressed the same as the suspects. After the user retweeted the photo, other people jumped in to identify the restaurant where it was taken, and another researched the patrons who had used Facebook's check-in feature at that location. The perpetrators were among them. Due to these efforts, two men and a woman were identified and convicted of assault.

In some cases, officers compare data gleaned from social networking profiles against police records and phone records to identify elusive members of organized crime networks. One operation in Cincinnati led to the arrests of seventy-one gang affiliates. To lure criminals offline, authorities may create fake social media accounts. An agent highlights one anecdote: "We contacted a guy [on social media] that had been involved in a homicide two days prior. We set up a date with him and let him pick the location, because we couldn't find him and wanted to arrest him on federal gun and drug charges and interview him about the murder. He showed up and we arrested him."[68] Besides catching known suspects, agents can cast a wider net by impersonating children in order to catch pedophiles or pose as someone looking for drugs to nab dealers.

Self-Incrimination

Sometimes wrongdoers make an investigator's job easy—by incriminating themselves. Social media messages alone are not usually admissible as evidence in court, but they often provide the necessary clues for police to crack a case. For example, in 2016 three burglars in Florida videotaped themselves bragging about a safe full of jewelry worth $500,000 that they had stolen. The men exclaimed on video, "We got a safe!" and "Can someone say check please?"[69] Reuters reporter Melissa Fares explains what happened next: "Raderius Glenn Collins was arrested in Pinecrest, Florida after he uploaded a 7-minute video to Facebook in May. He may have been happy to see his video get 3,000 views, but probably unhappy one of them was the police."[70] Thanks to the video, authorities tracked down the store where the men pawned the items as well as all three suspects—and found evidence linking them to another robbery, too.

Prevention of Suicides and Mass Killings

If someone is posting suicide notes or threatening to hurt others, social networkers can offer instant support. In one case, more than fifty members of Reddit sent supportive messages that convinced a teenager not to kill himself and to get psychiatric help. Some social media sites, such as Facebook and Twitter, reach out to suicidal users with resources and encouragement to seek help. One police officer reports how this saved someone's life: "Tip from social media user led to medical and mental assistance to a teen who had ingested excess medication in suicide attempt. Discovered via Tumblr."[71]

Social media has also played a role in preventing school shootings and bombings. Users can flag alarming posts for review by social media site administrators or share them with school authorities. Often this has resulted in students being apprehended and offered mental health services. At a high school in Fairfield, California, a fifteen-year-old student tweeted that he would hurt classmates at school the next day and included a photo of himself holding a rifle. A student told a parent, who contacted police that same night. Thanks to collaboration between school officials and police, the student was arrested at home less than three hours later, and the gun was confiscated before anyone was harmed.

Besides relying on tips from students, schools are taking a more active role in monitoring social media posts for keywords like *gun* to identify threats. Some employ sophisticated software that analyzes the context of messages and can distinguish between posts like "I bombed the test" and "I plan to bomb the school." Scott Anderle, a Glendale, California, school district official, asserts, "We've actually prevented a number—is it a huge number, no—but a number of incidents where kids were either thinking about killing themselves or doing something bad to the school and we were able to get involved and stop that from happening."[72]

> "We've actually prevented a number . . . of incidents where kids were either thinking about killing themselves or doing something bad to the school."[72]
>
> —Scott Anderle, a Glendale, California, school district official

Many Uses as a Crime-Fighting Tool

Perhaps most significant is social media's ability to reach potentially billions of people, making it possible to aid law enforcement agencies around the globe. Today's technology allows anyone to snap a photo of a suspicious person or a suspect's license plate and allows police to disseminate this information to wide networks instantly. This aids victims, brings criminals to justice, and makes communities safer.

Social Networking Fuels Crime and Violence

"Criminals trawl social media constantly, looking for vulnerabilities and vacations, pinpointing easy targets."

—Theodore F. Claypoole, a cybersecurity lawyer

Theodore F. Claypoole, "Privacy and Social Media," *Business Law Today*, January 2014. www.americanbar.org.

Consider these questions as you read:

1. Do you agree with the claim that bullying can be more troubling on social networking sites than in person? Why or why not?
2. Do you believe that social networking sites encourage users to share too much personal information? Explain your answer.
3. Do you agree with the assertion that the increasing number of hate group "likes" is connected to the rise in hate crimes? Why or why not?

Editor's note: The discussion that follows presents common arguments made in support of this perspective, reinforced by facts, quotes, and examples taken from various sources.

On social networking sites, millions of people share personal information about themselves that they would never reveal in public. This provides a wealth of opportunities for predators seeking victims online, where anonymity allows them to fly under the radar. Worse, the crimes can go beyond the Internet into the real world, as when criminals stalk or attack people they initially found on social networking sites. Not to mention that due to live streaming, anyone with a social media account can now accidentally witness crimes happening in real time, including suicides, rapes, and murders that people have streamed. All of these occurrences make social media sites dangerous for anyone, especially young people.

Cyberbullying

For years, Texas teenager Brandy Vela endured bullying over her weight, but in 2016 it got much worse. An unknown perpetrator began to send insulting messages to her cell phone. Then someone impersonated her through a fake social media profile that displayed her name and phone number with lewd messages asking people to call her for sex. Each time she reported it, the site would shut down the page, but another profile would soon open. Her high school's deputy investigated, but the messages were untraceable and continued even after Vela changed her number. Meanwhile, strangers who got her number online messaged her constantly. Then the bully shared sexually explicit photos of her on social media. According to her family, "The harsh messages and fake social media pages created to bully and impersonate her became too much for her to handle."[73] That November, she killed herself. Even then, her Facebook memorial page was peppered with horrible comments "congratulating" her. Finally, months later, police arrested her twenty-one-year-old ex-boyfriend and his new girlfriend on suspicion of her bullying.

> "The harsh messages and fake social media pages created to bully and impersonate her became too much for her to handle."[73]
>
> —The family of Brandy Vela, a teenager who committed suicide after being cyberbullied

Sadly, many young people like Vela are viciously cyberbullied, or harassed through electronic communication. According to a survey by the Pew Research Center, 55 percent of teens who use social media have witnessed cyberbullying there, and nearly all of them did nothing in response. Bullying is not new, of course, but it is especially problematic in today's social networking world. For one thing, it is easy for anyone to type terrible insults from a computer or phone, even if they would never verbally or physically hurt someone in person. Secondly, cyberbullies' identities can be kept anonymous, as in Vela's case. Another issue is that in the past, school bullying would stop at least temporarily while the student was home, but now social networking provides constant access to the person being bullied. Harassment can occur day or night in all sorts of ways—through a group chat, sharing embarrassing photos, or even a YouTube channel devoted to insulting someone. Disturbingly, a 2017 survey in the United Kingdom by the antibullying organization Ditch the Label found that 26 percent of young people who were cyberbullied have considered suicide. In addition, 71 percent believe social networking sites do not do enough to combat cyberbullying. The sites could monitor for bullying and suspend cyberbullies' accounts, for example.

Privacy-Related Crimes

Social networking sites are not designed for people to shield information about themselves—quite the opposite. They encourage users to share as much as possible, putting them at risk of becoming crime victims. "The business model development for social media sites is designed to coerce, cajole, trick, taunt, or tease us into revealing more information about our lives and our thoughts and opinions,"[74] cybersecurity lawyer Theodore F. Claypoole says. That is because the sites are paid for the data they collect about all of their users, which is analyzed, sold, and resold to data mining companies and advertisers.

> "Social media sites [are] designed to coerce, cajole, trick, taunt, or tease us into revealing more information about our lives and our thoughts and opinions."[74]
>
> —Theodore F. Claypoole, a corporate attorney who specializes in cybersecurity

All of this storage and transfer of information provides multiple points for data breaches and identity theft. According to Simon Dukes, chief executive of the fraud-prevention service Cifas, "The likes of Facebook, Twitter, LinkedIn and other online platforms are much more than just social media sites—they are now a hunting ground for identity thieves."[75] Though social network users do have the ability to set stricter privacy controls, the National Crime Prevention Council and other groups caution that even if account settings are set to private, users are still at risk of their accounts being hacked.

Sharing of personal data and real-time location check-ins allow criminals to stalk or burglarize social media users offline, too. In fact, 78 percent of burglars admit they use social media to seek victims. When people post that they are on vacation or at another location, their empty home becomes a target. Savvy burglars can identify the address through online searches or from geotagging, a feature that displays the exact location where each photo was taken. In Orange County, California, one criminal identified at least thirty-three college women at malls and coffee shops, used their social media check-ins to find and track them online, got their home addresses from geotagged photos, and stole $250,000 worth of items from them.

Sexual Predators

Even worse, social networking attracts sexual predators who scour photos of potential victims. From 2009 to 2013, sexual assaults linked to Facebook and Twitter in the United Kingdom increased by 342 percent, and many of these victims were under age sixteen. One police officer reasons, "We know that some sex offenders will wander the streets looking for vulnerable people late at night. But there is absolutely no reason to think they won't spend time online doing exactly the same."[76]

Young people are at risk of connecting with pedophiles, who can easily lie about their name, gender, or age. In one study of Internet-related sex crimes committed against minors, 69 percent of the abusers gleaned information from their victim's social media profile. Using details from social networking, predators build rapport by telling minors "how pretty they are, how smart they are, how handsome, how good they are at school. Once they gain the trust of that child . . . they start asking for pictures and videos of these kids naked,"[77] explains FBI agent John Letterhos. If young people do send a photo, it may be used to blackmail them into sending more photos or videos. Eventually the perpetrators may ask to meet in person, and that is when they are likely to commit assault. Obviously, young people must be protected from these dangers.

Hate Crimes

Another adverse effect of social media is it gives a platform to hate groups composed of people who are racist or prejudiced. From 2014 to 2016,

Cyberbullying Makes Social Networks Dangerous

Cyberbullying (also known as electronic harassment) is a crime in all but two states. The sad fact is that social networking sites give bullies a convenient platform for targeting their victims. This is exemplified in research by Ditch the Label, an antibullying nonprofit in the United Kingdom that surveyed more than ten thousand young people between the ages of twelve and twenty. The results reveal a surprising number of people have been bullied on social media. In addition, most respondents believe social networks do not do enough to protect users from cyberbullying, and only 6 percent say social networks are safe.

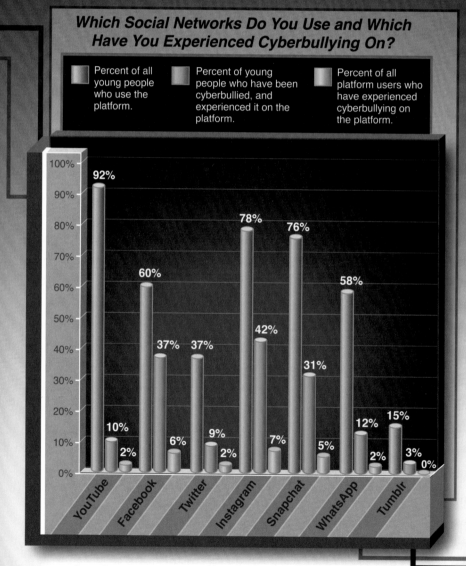

Which Social Networks Do You Use and Which Have You Experienced Cyberbullying On?

- Percent of all young people who use the platform.
- Percent of young people who have been cyberbullied, and experienced it on the platform.
- Percent of all platform users who have experienced cyberbullying on the platform.

Platform	Use	Been cyberbullied	Platform users
YouTube	92%	10%	2%
Facebook	60%	37%	6%
Twitter	37%	9%	2%
Instagram	78%	42%	7%
Snapchat	76%	31%	5%
WhatsApp	58%	12%	2%
Tumblr	15%	3%	0%

Source: Ditch the Label, "Annual Bullying Survey 2017," July 2017. www.ditchthelabel.org.

the number of "likes" on hate group tweets and comments increased tenfold. Even more concerning, some people go beyond simply joining a hate group. FBI data reveals there were 5,818 hate crimes against racial minorities, women, gays, and others in 2015, about 6 percent more than the previous year. One case in 2017 exemplifies the connection between social media hate groups and crime. After a white man allegedly stabbed black army lieutenant Richard W. Collins III to death at the University of Maryland, investigators discovered something in the suspect's social media account. He was a member of a white supremacist Facebook group called Alt-Reich Nation. Police described the group as "despicable, it shows extreme bias against women, Latinos, members of the Jewish faith and especially African Americans."[78] It is no coincidence that many people who commit hate crimes also belong to hateful social media groups.

Not Enough Regulation

Following the murder of Collins, one concerned citizen tweeted, "Facebook needs to shut down #altReich hate groups. They mobilize and embolden racist idiots."[79] Yet most social networks do not censor hate speech or hate groups. For one thing, hate speech is generally protected under the First Amendment. For another, the federal Telecommunications Act of 1996 specifies that most technology companies, including Facebook, are not legally responsible for the content their users post and thus are not obligated to censor content. That means the dangers posed by social networking are here to stay for the foreseeable future.

Source Notes

Overview: Social Networking

1. *Dim Mak* (blog), "Unplugged: Spent 24 Hours Without Technology and Survived, Barely," February 29, 2016. www.dimmak.com.
2. Quoted in Nancy Jo Sales, *American Girls: Social Media and the Secret Lives of Teenagers*. New York: Knopf, 2016, p. 9.
3. Farhad Manjoo, "Social Media's Globe-Shaking Power," *New York Times*, November 16, 2016. www.nytimes.com.
4. Donald Trump, interviewed by Lesley Stahl, *60 Minutes*, CBS News, November 13, 2016. www.cbsnews.com.
5. Karen Yankovich, "How Social Media Won an Election and Shocked the World," Social Media Today, November 17, 2016. www.socialmediatoday .com.
6. Quoted in Joseph Weber, "Trump Recruiting 'Election Observers' to Scout for Fraud," Fox News, August 17, 2016. www.foxnews.com.
7. Quoted in Eric Johnson, "Full Transcript: Hillary Clinton at Code 2017," Recode, May 31, 2017. www.recode.net.

Chapter One: Does Social Networking Benefit Society?

8. AJ Agrawal, "It's Not All Bad: The Social Good of Social Media," *Forbes*, March 18, 2016. www.forbes.com.
9. Pulse Orlando's Facebook page, June 11, 2016. www.facebook.com.
10. Quoted in Henri Gendreau, "The Internet Made 'Fake News' a Thing—Then Made It Nothing," *Wired*, February 25, 2017. www.wired.com.
11. Mustafa Nayyem, "Uprising in Ukraine: How It All Began," Open Society Foundations, April 4, 2014. www.opensocietyfoundations.com.
12. Arseniy Yatsenyuk, Twitter, January 25, 2014. www.twitter.com.
13. Joshua A. Tucker et al., "Protest in the Age of Social Media," *Carnegie Reporter*, Fall 2014. www.medium.com.
14. Women's March Washington State, "About: National Mission Statement." www.womensmarchwastate.org.
15. Melanie Pinola, *LinkedIn in 30 Minutes: How to Create a Rock-Solid Linked-In Profile and Build Connections That Matter*. Newton, MA: i30 Media Corporation, 2013, p. 4.
16. Malcolm Cox and *Advertising Week*, "Honesty on Social Media Just May Be the Best Policy," *Huffington Post*, July 22, 2016. www.huffingtonpost.com.

17. Geri Stengel, "Why Crowdfunding Is a Game-Change for Women Entrepreneurs," *Forbes*, January 30, 2013. www.forbes.com.
18. Lucy Goodchild van Hilten, "Debunking Zika Virus Pseudoscience: We Need to Respond Fast, Say Researchers," Elsevier Connect, May 24, 2016. www.elsevier.com.
19. Filippo Menczer, "Misinformation on Social Media: Can Technology Save Us?," Conversation, November 27, 2016. www.theconversation.com.
20. Quoted in Scott Pelley, "How Fake News Becomes a Popular, Trending Topic," *60 Minutes*, CBS, March 26, 2017. www.cbsnews.com.
21. Nick Wingfield et al., "Google and Facebook Take Aim at Fake News Sites," *New York Times*, November 14, 2016. www.nytimes.com.
22. Quoted in Linda L. Lyman, ed., *Brain Science for Principals: What School Leaders Need to Know*. Lanham, MD: Rowman & Littlefield, 2016, p. 32.
23. Neal Samudre, "8 Dangers of Social Media We're Not Willing to Admit," *Relevant*, April 19, 2016. www.relevantmagazine.com.
24. Matt Cutts, "When You've Got 5 Minutes to Fill, Twitter Is a Great Way to Fill 35 Minutes," Twitter, May 10, 2010. www.twitter.com.
25. Bindi Donnelly, "How Facebook Subtly Works to Reinforce Your Prejudices, Without You Even Realising," Junkee, May 22, 2015. www.junkee.com.
26. Ronald Alsop, "Instant Gratification & Its Dark Side," *Bucknell Magazine*, Summer 2014. www.bucknell.edu.

Chapter Two: Does Social Networking Weaken People's Social Skills?

27. Lexi Herrick, "11 Things We Fake in Our Social Media Lives," *Huffington Post*, June 30, 2016. www.huffingtonpost.com.
28. Jay Baer, "Social Media, Pretend Friends, and the Lie of False Intimacy," *Convince & Convert* (blog). www.convinceandconvert.com.
29. R.I.M. Dunbar, "Do Online Social Media Cut Through the Constraints That Limit the Size of Offline Social Networks?," *Royal Society Open Science*, January 2016. http://rsos.royalsocietypublishing.org.
30. Ann Smarty, "Social Media and Society: The Good, the Bad, and the Ugly," Seochat. www.seochat.com.
31. Behrouz Jafarnezhad, "Social Media: Does It Connect or Disconnect People in Real Life?," *Perspective IX* (blog), November 7, 2015. http://perspectiveix.com.
32. Jafarnezhad, "Social Media."
33. Quoted in University of Pittsburgh Health Sciences Media Relations, "More Social Connection Online Tied to Increasing Feelings of Isolation," ScienceDaily, March 6, 2017. www.sciencedaily.com.

34. Quoted in Kate Moriarty, "Are Social Media Making You Depressed?," Her Campus, June 15, 2016. www.hercampus.com.
35. Quoted in Chandra Johnson, "Face Time vs. Screen Time: The Technological Impact on Communication," *Salt Lake City (UT) Deseret News*, August 29, 2014. www.deseretnews.com.
36. Quoted in Michael Sliney, "Social Media Worries for Your Kids? Maybe Put Your Own Phone Down First," Fox News, January 31, 2017. www.foxnews.com.
37. Emily Alampi, "How Social Media May Be Damaging Your Relationship," Odyssey, January 25, 2016. www.theodysseyonline.com.
38. Quoted in Jennifer Lau, *Social Intelligence and the Next Generation*. London: National Citizen Service/King's College London, 2016, p. 24.
39. Adelle Waldman, "Shyness Is Nice (Except on Social Media)," *Vogue*, June 25, 2014. www.vogue.com.
40. Barry Birkett, "5 Benefits of Social Media for Seniors—Let's Help Them Get Online!," Senior Care Corner. www.seniorcarecorner.com.
41. Sofia Kaliarnta, "Using Aristotle's Theory of Friendship to Classify Online Friendships: A Critical Counterview," *Ethics and Information Technology*, June 2016, p. 78.
42. Melinda Ring, "Teen Depression and How Social Media Can Help or Hurt," CNN, August 6, 2015. www.cnn.com.
43. Quoted in Ring, "Teen Depression and How Social Media Can Help or Hurt."
44. Ring, "Teen Depression and How Social Media Can Help or Hurt."
45. Gwendolyn Seidman, "Can You Really Trust the People You Meet Online?," *Close Encounters* (blog), *Psychology Today*, July 23, 2014. www.psychologytoday.com.
46. Quoted in Laura Donovan, "Why More People Should Embrace the Real Side of Instagram," ATTN:, December 2, 2015. www.attn.com.
47. Quoted in Carrie Kerpen, "How Has Social Media Changed Us?," *Forbes*, April 21, 2016. www.forbes.com.

Chapter Three: Is Social Networking Harming Young People?

48. Benjamin Gordon, "Social Media Is Ruining Everything," *Huffington Post*, May 11, 2016. www.huffingtonpost.com.
49. Rachael Tulipano, "Brief Happiness: The Truth Behind Why We Want Instant Gratification," Elite Daily, September 1, 2015. www.elitedaily.com.
50. Quoted in BBC, "Instagram 'Worst for Young Mental Health,'" May 19, 2017. www.bbc.com.

51. Quoted in Rebecca Granet, "Living in Live Time: Social Media's Impact on Girls," CBS New York, September 19, 2016. http://newyork.cbslocal.com.

52. Quoted in Minas Michikyan et al., "Facebook Use and Academic Performance Among College Students: A Mixed-Methods Study with a Multi-ethnic Sample," *Computers in Human Behavior*, April 2015, p. 268.

53. Quoted in Aly Weisman, "Louis C.K. Rants About 'Toxic' Cell Phones Distracting People from Feeling Sadness," Business Insider, September 20, 2013. www.businessinsider.com.

54. Quoted in Michelle Meyers, "How Instagram Became the Social Network for Tweens," CNET, September 8, 2012. www.cnet.com.

55. Naomi Schaefer Riley, "Don't Downplay the Dangers of Social Media to Kids," *New York Post*, February 7, 2016. www.nypost.com.

56. Quoted in Kelly Wallace, "The Upside of Selfies: Social Media Isn't All Bad for Kids," CNN, October 7, 2014. www.cnn.com.

57. Quoted in Wallace, "The Upside of Selfies: Social Media Isn't All Bad for Kids."

58. Quoted in *Today*/AOL, "Ideal to Real Body Image Survey," Scribd, February 2014. www.scribd.com.

59. Quoted in Susie East, "Teens: This Is How Social Media Affects Your Brain," CNN, August 1, 2016. www.cnn.com.

60. Larry D. Rosen, "The Power of 'Like,'" *Rewired: The Psychology of Technology* (blog), *Psychology Today*, July 15, 2012. www.psychologytoday.com.

61. Rusul Alrubail, "Social Media & Students' Communication Skills," Edutopia, July 14, 2015. www.edutopia.org.

62. Rebecca Mix Yard, "Technology and Social Media in Motivating At-Risk High School Students to Complete High School," Walden University ScholarWorks, 2015. http://scholarworks.waldenu.edu.

63. Jacqui Cheng, "What Inner City Kids Know About Social Media, and Why We Should Listen," *Medium* (blog), September 25, 2013. www.medium.com.

Chapter Four: Does Social Networking Facilitate Crime and Violence?

64. National Crime Prevention Council, "Can You Twitter Crime Away?," August 11, 2009. http://ncpc.typepad.com.

65. Quoted in Drew Kann, "A Decade Later, Where the Search for Madeleine McCann Stands," CNN, May 5, 2017. www.cnn.com.

66. Mark Zuckerberg's Facebook page, May 26, 2015. www.facebook.com.

67. Quoted in Alex Hagan, "Social Media Solves Three Crimes in Palm Beach County," WPTV, June 25, 2016. www.wptv.com.

68. Quoted in LexisNexis, "Social Media Use in Law Enforcement: Crime Prevention and Investigative Activities Continue to Drive Usage," November 2014. www.lexisnexis.com.

69. Quoted in Melissa Fares, "Florida Man Brags About Burglary on Facebook, Lands Him in Jail," Reuters, June 23, 2016. www.reuters.com.

70. Fares, "Florida Man Brags About Burglary on Facebook, Lands Him in Jail."

71. Quoted in LexisNexis, "Social Media Use in Law Enforcement."

72. Quoted in Malena Carollo, "The Secretive Industry of Social Media Monitoring," *Christian Science Monitor*, November 16, 2015. www.csmonitor.com.

73. Quoted in Christopher Brennan, "Ex-Boyfriend Arrested for Sharing Nude Photos of Texas Teen Who Killed Self After Cyberbullying," *New York Daily News*, March 16, 2017. www.nydailynews.com.

74. Theodore F. Claypoole, "Privacy and Social Media," *Business Law Today*, January 2014. www.americanbar.org.

75. Quoted in Sarah Samee, "Criminals Target UK Youth as Identity Fraud Rises," press release, Cifas, July 4, 2016. www.cifas.uk.org.

76. Quoted in Tom Pettifor, "Facebook Sex Crimes Soar: Offences via Social Networks More than Quadruple in Last Four Years," *Mirror* (London), April 1, 2013. www.mirror.co.uk.

77. Quoted in Jonathan Rodriguez, "More Sexual Predators Using Social Media to Lure Children, FBI Says," CBS North Carolina, July 21, 2016. www.wncn.com.

78. Quoted in *USA Today*, "FBI Investigating Possible Hate Crime at University of Maryland: What Is the 'Alt Reich: Nation' Facebook Group?," May 22, 2017. www.usatoday.com.

79. Quoted in *USA Today*, "FBI Investigating Possible Hate Crime at University of Maryland."

Social Networking Facts

Social Networking Usage

- The 2017 report *Digital in 2017: Global Overview* revealed that the country that uses social media the most is the Philippines, where users spend an average of four hours and seventeen minutes each day social networking.
- According to the Pew Research Center in 2016, 79 percent of all Americans who use the Internet have Facebook accounts. The majority of people who use Facebook (76 percent) log in at least once every day. For Instagram, 51 percent use it daily.
- According to Facebook cofounder Mark Zuckerberg, the platform had 2 billion users as of 2017.
- In 2016 Brandwatch, which conducts social media analytics, reviewed social media posts made over a six-month period and found nearly forty thousand people on Twitter who admitted being addicted to social media. Of all the posts admitting addiction, 32 percent were on Twitter, 20 percent were on Facebook, and 18 percent were on YouTube.
- In the last three months of 2016, Facebook made an average of $19.81 in advertising revenue for each user in the United States and Canada.

Young People on Social Networking Sites

- When a small group of students at Santa Clara University were polled in 2016, 42 percent said they had limited the number of friends or connections they had on social media due to privacy concerns.
- In a 2015 study by CNN, more than a third of middle schoolers admitted they purposely excluded others online, and 94 percent of parents underestimated the amount of fighting that occurs on social networking.
- CNN also found in 2015 that some teens take two hundred selfies before deciding which one to post on social media.

- In a 2015 survey by the Pew Research Center, 88 percent of teens who use social networking reported that their peers share too much information about themselves.
- According to a report in 2016 by the National Cyber Security Alliance, 54 percent of parents claim they have a household rule that their teens cannot join new social networks without their permission, but only 16 percent of teens said they have this rule.
- A poll by CauseVox in 2016 found that 61 percent of millennials (born from 1980 to 2000) posted on social media about causes they care about at least once in the previous week. The site they most commonly used was Facebook, followed by Twitter, and then Instagram.

Negative Effects

- According to British fraud-prevention service Cifas, social media is partly to blame for identity theft increasing in Brits under age thirty. It rose by 52 percent from 2014 to 2015.
- More than half of people surveyed by mobile phone company HTC in 2015 said they post images on social media just to make friends and family jealous, and 6 percent admitted they have taken a photo of someone else's belongings and shared it on social media as though the belongings were their own.
- According to a University of Pittsburgh School of Medicine study released in 2016, more than 80 percent of people had at least one negative experience on Facebook, and 60 percent had four or more. In addition, those who reported using seven to eleven social media platforms had more than three times the risk of depression and anxiety than those who used zero to two platforms.
- In 2017 Facebook removed about 66,000 posts a week, or about 288,000 a month, for being too hateful or directly inciting violence.
- Research by the cybersecurity company Symantec found that in 2014, 70 percent of social media scams with links to outside sites were voluntarily and unwittingly shared by users, compared to only 2 percent in 2013.

Positive Effects

- According to the Pew Research Center in 2015, 29 percent of people aged thirteen to seventeen have made more than five new friends online. Of those who met a friend online, the most common source is social media (64 percent).
- A survey by CareerBuilder in 2015 found that one-third of employers who visited a job candidate's profile discovered information that prompted them to hire the candidate.
- In February 2011 political protest fueled by social media culminated in Egyptian president Hosni Mubarak stepping down. The week before, Twitter logged about 230,000 tweets every day about protest in Egypt, up from only 2,300 per day before that, and the top 23 videos about political change in Egypt were watched by 5.5 million viewers.
- According to the National Center for Missing & Exploited Children, 98.5 percent of AMBER Alerts were resolved and recovered from 2005 to 2009, in part due to social media.
- For an art project exhibited in 2017, photographer Tanja Hollander contacted all 626 of her Facebook friends, some of whom she had never met, and asked to travel to their home and photograph their family. An astounding 95 percent of them invited her to do so, and 74 percent provided her a meal or overnight lodging in their home, suggesting that they trusted her as a real friend.

Related Organizations and Websites

Center for Safe and Responsible Internet Use
474 W. Twenty-Ninth Ave.
Eugene, OR 97405
e-mail: contact@csriu.org • website: www.cyberbully.org

The Center for Safe and Responsible Internet Use works to help young people keep themselves safe and respect others on the Internet. Its website has numerous reports designed to help people learn about responsible Internet behavior, including a series of cyberbullying guides geared toward students, parents, and educators.

Common Sense Media
650 Townsend St., Suite 435
San Francisco, CA 94103
website: www.commonsensemedia.org

Common Sense Media is an organization that believes all forms of media have a profound influence on youth and was created in order to help educate families about these effects. It offers the information and tools people need to make educated choices about their media use, including a wealth of statistics and studies concerning social networking.

Cyberbullying Research Center
website: www.cyberbullying.us

The Cyberbullying Research Center is a clearinghouse of information about cyberbullying. It provides information about the nature, extent, causes, and consequences of cyberbullying among teens. The website contains numerous statistics about this issue and stories from youths who have been affected by cyberbullying.

Electronic Frontier Foundation (EFF)
815 Eddy St.
San Francisco, CA 94109
e-mail: information@eff.org • website: www.eff.org

Founded in 1990, the EFF is a nonprofit organization that seeks to defend various civil liberties in relation to telecommunications technologies such as the Internet. Its website has news and reports about free speech, privacy, and political advocacy as related to social networking.

GetNetWise
e-mail: tlordan@neted.org • website: www.getnetwise.org

GetNetWise is a website provided by Internet industry corporations and public interest organizations. Its goal is to ensure that Internet users have safe and constructive online experiences. The website contains information for both youth and parents about social networking, youth safety, security, and privacy.

Internet Society (ISOC)
1775 Wiehle Ave., Suite 201
Reston, VA 20190
e-mail: isoc@isoc.org • website: www.internetsociety.org

The ISOC is an international nonprofit group that works to ensure the open development of the Internet for the benefit of people throughout the world. Its website has information about social networking and privacy issues.

National Cyber Security Alliance (NCSA)
1010 Vermont Ave. NW
Washington, DC 20005
website: www.staysafeonline.org

The National Cyber Security Alliance is a nonprofit organization that works to empower the online community to be safe and secure. It offers resources for Internet users, parents, and educators on a variety of topics, including online bullying, stalking, and impersonation.

Pew Internet & American Life Project

1615 L St. NW, Suite 700

Washington, DC 20036

e-mail: info@pewinternet.org • website: http://pewinternet.org

The Pew Internet & American Life Project studies how Americans use the Internet and how digital technologies are shaping the world today. Numerous studies on social networking are available on its website.

WiredSafety

website: www.wiredsafety.org

Founded in 1995, WiredSafety is a nonprofit group that works to educate people of all ages about online safety. Its website features information about numerous safety issues, including cyberbullying, privacy, and Internet crime.

For Further Research

Books

danah boyd, *It's Complicated: The Social Lives of Networked Teens*. New Haven, CT: Yale University Press, 2014.

Christian Fuchs, *Social Media: A Critical Introduction*. 2nd ed. Los Angeles: Sage, 2017.

Sameer Hinduja and Justin W. Patchin, *Bullying Beyond the Schoolyard: Preventing and Responding to Cyberbullying*. 2nd ed. Thousand Oaks, CA: Corwin, 2014.

Regina Luttrell, *Social Media: How to Engage, Share, and Connect*. 2nd ed. Lanham, MD: Rowman & Littlefield, 2016.

Nancy Jo Sales, *American Girls: Social Media and the Secret Lives of Teenagers*. New York: Knopf, 2016.

Sherry Turkle, *Reclaiming Conversation: The Power of Talk in a Digital Age*. New York: Penguin, 2015.

Internet Sources

Lenzi Causey, "Is Social Media Ruining Our Communication Skills?," Odyssey, August 1, 2016. www.theodysseyonline.com/social-media-affecting-communication-skills.

Ditch the Label, "Annual Bullying Survey 2017," July 2017. www.ditchthelabel.org/research-papers/the-annual-bullying-survey-2017.

Laura Donovan, "Why More People Should Embrace the Real Side of Instagram," ATTN:, December 2, 2015. www.attn.com/stories/4384/honesty-on-instagram.

Rebecca Granet, "Living in Live Time: Social Media's Impact on Girls," CBS New York, September 19, 2016. http://newyork.cbslocal.com /2016/09/19/social-media-use-teens.

Bobby Hoffman, "Research Reveals New Risks for Daily Social Media Users," *Motivate!* (blog), *Psychology Today*, November 13, 2015. www .psychologytoday.com/blog/motivate/201511/research-reveals-new -risks-daily-social-media-users.

Carrie Kerpen, "How Has Social Media Changed Us?," *Forbes*, April 21, 2016. www.forbes.com/sites/carriekerpen/2016/04/21/how-has-social -media-changed-us/#619803b85dfc.

Felicity Morse, "How Social Media Helped Me Deal with My Mental Illness," BBC, February 18, 2016. www.bbc.co.uk/newsbeat/article /35607567/how-social-media-helped-me-deal-with-my-mental-illness.

Suren Ramasubbu, "Influence of Social Media on Teenagers," *Huffington Post*, May 26, 2016. www.huffingtonpost.com/suren-ramasubbu/influ ence-of-social-media-on-teenagers_b_7427740.html.

Gwendolyn Seidman, "Can You Really Trust the People You Meet Online?," *Close Encounters* (blog), *Psychology Today*, July 23, 2014. www.psych ologytoday.com/blog/close-encounters/201407/can-you-really-trust -the-people-you-meet-online.

Christopher Soghoian, "Why Online Privacy Matters—and How to Protect Yours," Ideas.Ted.com., August 9, 2016. http://ideas.ted.com/why -online-privacy-matters-and-how-to-protect-yours.

Shankar Vedantam, "Why Social Media Isn't Always Very Social," Morning Edition, NPR, May 2, 2017. www.npr.org/2017/05/02/526514168 /why-social-media-isnt-always-very-social.

Teddy Wayne, "Found on Facebook: Empathy," *New York Times*, October 9, 2015. www.nytimes.com/2015/10/11/fashion/found-on-facebook-em pathy.html?mcubz=1.

Index

Note: Boldface page numbers indicate illustrations.

52–53, **54**, 55, 56–57
learning problems, 42–43
Letterhos, John, 61
Levey, Rebecca, 46
LexisNexis, 52
LinkedIn, **15**, 17
Lovell, Nicole, 44

Manjoo, Farhad, 9
Masio, Eileen, 46
mass killings, 14–15, 56–57
McCann, Madeleine, 53
Menczer, Filippo, 20
Microsoft, 11, 21
middle schoolers, use by, 69
millennial generation
    destruction of patience, 40
    effect of round-the-clock connection, 24
    as "hooked" on, 6
    percent of
        getting news from social media, 14
        posting about causes, 17, 70
Mitchell, Clarence, 53
Mubarak, Hosni, 71
multitasking, 21, 42–43

National Center for Missing & Exploited
    Children, 53, 55, 71
National Crime Prevention Council, 53, 60
National Cyber Security Alliance, 43–44, 70
Nayyem, Mustafa, 16
news. *See* information
New York Times (newspaper), 21
NORC at the University of Chicago, 47

Olapic, 35

Patheja, Savina, 19
patience, destruction of, 40
pedophiles, 43–44, 61
Pew Research Center
    percent of American adults getting news from
        social media, 14
    percent of Americans using Internet with
        Facebook accounts, 69
    percent of teenagers
        concerned about peers' sharing information,
            69
        making friends online, 34, 71
        using, 7
        witnessing cyberbullying, 59
Philippines, 69
"phubbing," 29
Pinola, Melanie, 17
Pinterest, 7
platforms, types of, 7
political revolution, 16, 71
posts, as permanent, 7, 9
Powell-Lunder, Jennifer, 42
prejudice, social networking spreads, 19

hate groups on Twitter, **22**
increase in activity of hate groups, 23–24, 61,
    63
Primack, Brian, 29–30
privacy
    data collected by platforms and, 10–11, 70
    limiting number of friends due to concerns
        about, 69
    young people do not protect, 43–44
    young people protect, 49–50

racism. *See* prejudice, social networking spreads
Reddit, 7, 56
relationships. *See* social interactions and skills
revolutions, 16, 71
Riley, Naomi Schaefer, 44
Ring, Matthew, 36
Ring, Melinda, 36
Rosen, Larry D., 48–49
Roufa, Timothy, 52
Rutledge, Pamela, 46

Samudre, Neal, 26
Santa Clara University, 49–50, 69
Saudi Arabia, **8**
school performance, 43, 49
Seidman, Gwendolyn, 36–37
self-esteem
    social networking benefits, 45, 46–48, **47**
    social networking harms, **28**, 42, 59–60, **62**
selfies, 37, 42, 46, 69
self-incrimination, 56
Sentencing Project, 24
sexts, 42
sexual predators, 43–44, 61
Sherman, Lauren, 47–48
Silva, Clarissa, 28
60 Minutes (television program), 20
Smarty, Ann, 28
Snapchat
    cyberbullying on, **62**
    deletion of messages, 50
    negative effects of, on young people, 39, **41**
    used in hiring process, **15**
social campaigns, 17, 71
social interactions and skills
    by middle schoolers, 69
    percent posting to make others jealous, 70
    social networking hinders, 25
        comments result in misunderstandings, 31
        deterioration of communication skills,
            30–31, 43
        distracted from those nearby, 29
        friendships are superficial, 26, 27
        "phubbing," 29
        unreal versions of lives are posted, 26–27, 42
        users prone to isolation and depression,
            29–30
    social networking improves, 25
        ability to make new friends, 33–34

79